Seen, Un-Seen Disneyland
What You See at Disneyland, but Never Really See

Russell D. Flores

D0954188

2012
Synergy-Books Publishing, U.S.A.

Seen, Un-Seen Disneyland: What You See at
Disneyland, but Never Really See.
By Russell D. Flores

Published by
Synergy-Books Publishing
P.O. Box 911232
Saint George, UT 84791
www.synergy-books.com

All photography by Russell Flores

Written by Russell D. Flores

ISBN: 978-1-936434-48-0

Second Edition

10 9 8 7 6 5 4 3 2

Cover picture: The cover picture was taken by the author. Seven people
were removed from the image and the author's daughter was added.

DISCLAIMERS

DISCLAIMERS CONTINUED

Accuracy Disclaimer: While I have attempted to make every reasonable effort and take every reasonable precaution in the making of this publication to ensure its accuracy, the publisher and author assume no responsibility for errors or omissions. Neither is any liability assumed for damages resulting or alleged to result, either directly or indirectly from the use of the information contained in this publication. If you do not wish to be bound by these conditions, all books purchased from the publisher or its distributors may be returned this with receipt and in original new condition to the publisher for a full refund. All books purchased from third parties, such as eBay or a book store, should be returned to the third party. Every reasonable effort will be made by the publisher to refund your money if the third party refuses to refund your money.

Photograph Disclaimer: Every photograph was taken at Disneyland and is a true representation of what the photographer saw with the following exceptions: some images of guests have been blurred or photo edited out of the picture to protect their identity and /or their presence in the picture was distracting. Color enhancement, photo sharpening, and cropping were used to make some photos more presentable.

Disneyland is always trying to "Plus" (DL) their attractions (DL).Because of this, the book could not possibly keep up with all of the changes. Many items may be moved occasionally such as the coins setup in the shape of Mickey's head on the Pirate of the Caribbean. Look around to see if you can find it. And, unfortunately, some things may be removed, but rest assured that the Disney Imagineers (DL) have replaced it with another wonderful item.

ACKNOWLEDGEMENTS

I would like to take this time to thank all of the people who supported me in this endeavor.

Fellow Disney fans Kris, Valerie, and Brian Okamoto, and Jill and Scott Edwards for their review and input of this book. Their input really helped to make this book directed at the Disney fans.

Dave Smith (Chief Archivist Emeritus, The Walt Disney Archives) for graciously agreeing to be the first to review my book, and for helping make sure the book was accurate and used the proper "Disney Language." For him to take the time to review my book, gave me the confidence to complete my project. I have since had the opportunity to meet Mr. Smith several times including my first time at the Walt Disney Archives. He is just as gracious in-person as he was to correspond with by email.

Bill Cotter (author of *The Wonderful World of Disney Television*) for reviewing my book and providing me with great editorial feedback. His feedback really helped to make this a professional book.

David Oneal (Extinct Attractions/ThemeParks360.com) for his review, feedback, kind words of encouragement, and for introducing my book to the Disney community on his podcast.

The invaluable input and suggestions from these three men really helped to make this a polished, professional book.

Thomas "Tommy" Allison (Tommypix) for writing a great foreward.

David Smith of Synergy-Books Publishing for not only helping me to make this a better book, but for being my publisher.

Lynn Barron and Laura Gannon of The Sweep Spot podcast. They introduced me to David and Tommy.

David Lesjak Disney historian, author and professional copy editor for being so kind as to proof my book for this second edition.

I would especially like to thank my wife and daughter for their support and understanding, while taking pictures on our many trips and for allowing me the time to write this manuscript.

DEDICATION

I would like to dedicate this book to my wife and daughter, without whom this book would not exist. First, being great Disney fans, we spent a lot of time together at Disneyland, which allowed for all the pictures to be taken. Second, they were very patient and understanding when I needed to take pictures at the park. Third, they allowed me the time at home to research and compile my work and to ultimately write this book. And last, for pushing me to start printing my book. This book would not have come to fruition without their strong support.

TABLE OF CONTENTS

FOREWORD

Disneyland is a magical place that has layers of multiple surprises and experiences that captures our attention and excites our senses. Russell's new book reveals the back stories and the little details that you might not be aware of, that makes Disneyland so special. He has made multiple trips to the park to photograph and document his findings. As a annual passholder, who has been to the park over 250 times, I can tell you that I have learned many new things and was happy to revisit many familiar things to me. Seen, Un-Seen Disneyland will delight any Disney park enthusiast.

Thomas "Tommy" Allison aka @TommyPix
The DisGeek Podcast / The Sweep Spot Podcast

Introduction

Many people have gone to one or more of Disney's excellent theme parks. They have seen many wonderful and imaginative things. Disney Imagineers do a fantastic job. Everyone has seen the Castles and the Mountains, and many have found Hidden Mickeys (DL). Most have experienced the fun and thrilling attractions.

In November 2005, while on one of my many family trips to Disneyland, I was heading for the Big Thunder Mountain Railroad to meet up with my family. Big Thunder Mountain Railroad is one of our favorite attractions. I noticed a mother collect some trash from her children and throw it in a nearby waste can. I'm sure she did it without even giving a second thought as to how much detail Disney Imagineers put into the building and maintenance of all the Disney parks and attractions. I don't think she noticed that this was no ordinary waste can, for it was appropriately themed (DL) for Frontierland.

The waste can started as an ordinary waste can you find at many public venues, but its comparison ends there. It was painted to look like it was made of wooden boards, and the lettering was made to look like wood logs. I realized this was something I had never "Seen" before, even though I have been coming to the Park (DL) for over 46 years. I have probably used the waste cans at the Park hundreds, if not thousands of times. Still, this common object had remained an "Un-Seen" part of Disneyland for me. I marveled at how much thought the Disney Imagineers had put into not only this waste can but the whole Park. I took a quick picture, which I did not frame correctly, and continued onto Big Thunder Mountain Railroad.

While standing in line for Big Thunder Mountain Railroad, I began wondering how many other treasures there were at the Park that I had never "Seen." For the rest of the trip I started looking for other things I had never "Seen" before. I took several pictures including one of each type of waste can I saw. It got to be a family joke with the waste cans. Every time I started to take another picture, my daughter would say, "Mom, he's taking pictures of the waste cans again." At that point I hadn't told them about what I had noticed.

As I walked around the park on that trip, and many more times since, I was amazed at how many things I had never "Seen." I noticed things like a pedestrian crossing sign on Autopia that was actually a "Mouse Crossing" sign, and a "One Way" sign in Toontown that actually pointed both ways. I continued taking pictures and one day realized that other people may also be interested in a collection of pictures of this "Seen, Un-Seen Disneyland." I researched the topic and did not find any other books on Disneyland that covered this in detail. I decided to put my collection of photographs together in book format. The next question was, "What would the book consist of?"

First, I'll tell you what this book is not. It is not a behind-the-scenes book. It is not a Hidden Mickey book, although I may indulge in some. While I have been fortunate to see many things most guests never get or are suppose to see, this book is not a peek at the parts of Disneyland the Imagineers never intended guests (DL) to see. Some of the photographs have been intentionally cropped or masked in order to hide things I do not believe add to the photo or were not intended by the Disney Imagineers to be seen. I have also touched-up some photos to protect the identity of guests.

The intent of this book is <u>NOT</u> to destroy the "Disney Magic."

The intent of this book is to add to the enjoyment and memories of Disneyland. The book can be thought of as a guided tour to point out many of the wonderful and detailed sights that went into the making of Disneyland and which often go unnoticed. Some of the pictures show things you may have looked at several times and just didn't really see. Others may show things you have seen, but didn't know the backstory or history of the item. These are just a few of the elements that help make Disneyland the truly wonderful place it is.

This book contains the first sets of pictures that I hope to be a series of books not only on Disneyland, but all of the Disney parks. Each chapter contains pictures with a common theme. Since Disneyland was my first Disney park, and the one I have the most experience with, this book is on seen but un-seen Disneyland. I hope to do other books on Disney California Adventure, the Magic Kingdom, Disney's Hollywood Studios, EPCOT, and more.

Throughout the book, you will see (N:ZZZ), with ZZZ representing a number. This indicates there is a note. If you are interested, go to the notes chapter at the back of the book and locate the indicated number to discover the source or additional information.

The designation (DL) following a word, stands for "Disney Langauge" and denotes a word or phrase is commonly used in the Disney community. If you are unfamiliar with the word, please referance the Disney Language section at the back of the book for a short definition.

And to get started, I thought it only appropriate the first section in the book showcase those waste cans I first noticed that sunny day at Disneyland, and which provided the inspiration for this book.

Is That a Trash Can?

Keeping Disneyland Green

Most people who have been to Disneyland have used one or more waste/recycle cans. You finish a meal, drink or ice cream and diligently throw your trash into the nearest waste/recycle can. Disneyland has made sure there is always at least one waste can nearby. They were also one of the first theme parks to include recycle cans. Disneyland cast members even check the regular trash for recyclables before compacting the trash. But, have you stopped to look at them? I mean, really look at them? They are not just painted nice, they are painted to match the theme of the land or area they are in. They have their own show character named Push, and even have their own pin series. Can you guess where they are before reading the caption?

LEFT: In front of River Belle Terrace. The New Orleans Square and the Plaza Gardens Stage hosts many musical events. Note how the bars look like the inside of a piano or stringed instrument.

PREVIOUS PAGE: These waste cans were on the walkway between the Mark Twain/Columbia entrance and Big Thunder Mountain. Yes, this is the actual picture taken that fateful day. Notice how they are themed to the area to look like wood.

The trash can, like most in Disneyland, is paired with a recycle can. Disneyland was going "Green" before the term even existed. The recycle can, like many of the recycle cans around the park, that feature an image of Jiminy Cricket. In this case, he is our conscience to dump our recyclables in their proper place.

I apologize for the framing; it was taken in a hurry.

ABOVE: By Sleeping Beauty Castle, placed in front of a temporary fence during renovations. Note the classic depiction of a royal bird of prey.

Do you know approximately how many trash cans there are in Disneyland? (See note N: 114 for answer.)

LEFT: In front of It's a Small World, Fantasyland.

RIGHT: Fantasyland with that Pinocchio/Fantasyland, old-european look.

BELOW: Main Street U.S.A. with its classic old-town look.

RIGHT: They are even used for guard duty and crowd control. This can was in front of the Tiki Room exit in Adventureland. The waste can is made to look like stone.

ABOVE: Tomorrowland's very futuristic letter "T."

LEFT AND BELOW: Waste cans are so popular they have even been made into a show of their own. Here is a talking and walking (uh, rolling) waste can entertaining young and old alike. The character "Push" can be seen in various locations around Tomorrowland, and over at California Adventure.

LEFT: Even restaurants have themed waste cans. This one is located at the Pizza Port in Tomorrowland.

ABOVE AND RIGHT: Two types of waste cans sporting a jungle theme in Adventureland.

BELOW: In the Indiana Jones queue (DL). This can has a simple stone look with painted stencil lettering.

ABOVE: Haunted Mansion cans painted classic using the same green color used in Haunted Mansion cast member costumes.

ABOVE: In New Orleans Square with a New Orleans color and feel.

LEFT: Mickey's Toontown garbage can logo.

ABOVE AND BELOW: Even the waste cans in Mickey's Toontown can't escape the fun.

These cans are themed with the brooms from Fantasia and, of course, Jiminy Cricket.

ABOVE: ...and even a classic (outside the Park's main gates).

DISNEYLAND TRASH FACTS

1. Disneyland goes through 1,000 brooms, 500 dust pans and 3,000 mops per year.

2. They collect approximately 30 tons of trash per day or about 12 million tons per year.

3. Recycling per year (N: 89)
- 4.1 tons of cardboard.
- 1.3 million pounds of green waste.
- 370,000 pounds of office paper.
- 361,260 pounds of glass bottles.
- 274,280 pounds of plastic bottles.
- 17,240 pounds of aluminum cans.

4. In 2007, Disneyland successfully tested one of its train engines, which was converted to use a soy-based biofuel. Since that time, all of Disneyland's engines have been converted to this cleaner burning fuel. Just think, the next time you are riding one of the trains around Disneyland, the engine could be powered by the same oil used to cook your french fries. (N: 106)

An "E" Ticket Please...
The Ticket Booths

Many of the people who go to Disneyland today never had to use a ticket or ticket book. But back in the day, every attraction required a seperate ticket, and the best required an "E" ticket. This is where the phrase "E ticket ride" comes from. Those days are long gone and so are all of the ticket booths. At least that's what most people think. There are actually several ticket booths still in udse at the park, although they have been remodeled and/or re-purposed. Here are a few that you've probably seen several times, but may have never "Seen".

There were three types of ticket booths: Main Gate Ticket Booths sold ticket books with entry and attraction tickets; Central Ticket Booths located throughout the Park sold attraction tickets (A thru E); Attraction Ticket Booths collected the tickets. This chapter looks at old tickets booths still in use at Disneyland.

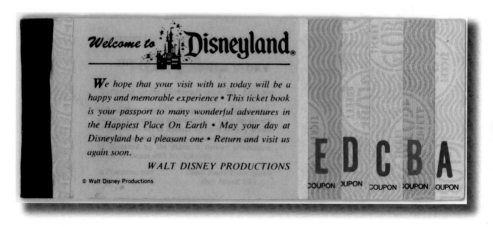

ABOVE: A common Junior ticket book that is part of my collection.

 It occured to me that many people have never seen a ticket or ticket book. There were many styles and types of tickets and ticket books.

On the this chapter's title page (previous page) are examples of several other types of tickets sold at the Park since its opening. The small beige-colored ticket with the E is an example of one of the first "E" tickets. This style of ticket was sold at the Central Ticket Booths throughout the park.

ABOVE: When Disneyland first opened, guests had to purchase both an entry ticket and tickets to the various attractions. In addition to the Main Gate Ticket Booths, guests could purchase additional attraction tickets at Central Ticket Booths located throughout the park. Prior to Disneyland discontinuing the use of tickets, this Kodak photo kiosk located by It's a Small World, was the Fantasyland central ticket sales booth. In 2013, Kodak discontinued its sponsorship. The booth currently sits empty waiting for a new assignment.(N: 1)

Attraction Ticket Booths were located at the entrances of any attraction requiring a ticket.

LEFT: The ticket booth at the Main Street Cinemas was actually used as an Attraction Ticket Booth. The booth now has a mannequin named Tilly who sits quietly. Cast members also collected tickets at the turnstiles. (N: 2)

RIGHT: The small train station in front of Casey Jr. used to be the attraction's ticket booth. (N: 5)

The lighthouse in front of the Storybookland attraction was an Attraction Ticket Booth. The ticket booth originally was located by Monstro. The line went from there into its present queue area. (N: 3)

LEFT: Its normal appearance today.

RIGHT: The lighthouse sporting a new gold paint job in honor Disneyland's 50th anniversary.

BELOW: One of the most popular "E" ticket attractions, and the first to be designated as such, is the Matterhorn Bobsleds. Guests originally purchased their tickets at one of the two windows prior to entering. Later, when they started the ticket book system, guests would hand their tickets to the ticket takers there. There are also windows on each side right at the turnstiles. Cast members also collected the tickets at the turnstiles. (N: 6)

The Bobsleds were the first tubular roller coaster ever built. This type of roller coaster is common today. (N: 7)

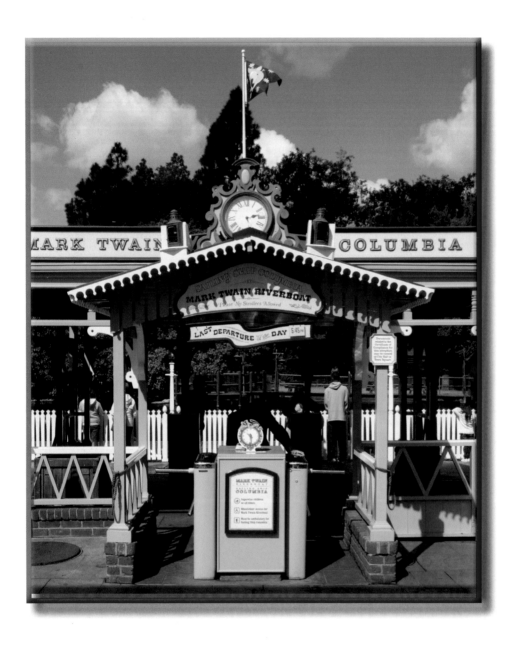

ABOVE: The center pedestal between the two turnstiles use to be a collection point for tickets at the Mark Twain/Columbia loading dock.

ABOVE: The mushroom in front of Alice in Wonderland was an Attraction Ticket Booth also. If you look at the mushroom while standing in line, that is the side the window was on. (N: 4)

ABOVE: The New Orleans/Frontierland Station used to just be the Frontierland Station. The building sat on the opposite side of the train tracks and was a working train station like the Main Street Station. In the early 1960s, the station moved across the tracks. and turned around 180 degrees. The side guests now see was originally the back side of the building. The window opposite the center window visible in this picture was the ticket window. The double doors opposite the ones visible were the entrance. These ones were the exit out onto the train platform.

Sleeping Beauty Castle

*O*ne of the most recognizable icons at the Park is Sleeping Beauty Castle. The castle is modeled after European castles, especially the Neuschwanstein castle in Bavaria. Everybody who comes to the park, sees the castle. Or do they? There are, of course, many things about the castle that people see everyday, but go unseen. (N: 90)

The book's cover picture shows the beautiful castle from the Central Plaza. Notice the wonderful detail, right down to the gold-colored paint on the spires. Actually, the spires are covered in 22-Karat gold leaf. This detail not only gives the castle the right color, but the gold leaf does not weather, making it cheaper in the long run to maintain. (N: 93)

In addition, have you you "Seen" the spire on the left side of the castle that wasn't completed? Some think it was missed, and others think it is a bad paint. Other guests think that this was done on purpose by Walt Disney as a symbol that "Disneyland will never be complete as long as there is Imagination left in the world." That is just an urban legend. Disney Imagineers actually tried a new patina process that they thought would last longer, but it didn't. (N: 94)

ABOVE AND RIGHT: Above the main entrance to the castle is a crest. Most guests don't really see the device, and those who do, might not realize crest represents the Disney family crest. (N: 8)

The drawbridge at the entrance to the Sleeping Beauty Castle actual works. Can you name the two times it was lowered? (See note N: 53 for answers.)

30

Placed beneath this marker on July 17, 1995:

The Disneyland 40th Anniversary Time Castle

A "Time Castle," containing Disneyland memories, messages and milestones, lies beneath this spot. The Disneyland Time Castle is dedicated to the children of the 21st century, who may unlock its contents on the 80th Anniversary of Disneyland: July 17, 2035.

ABOVE: The dedication plaque for the 40th anniversary time capsule buried at the Sleeping Beauty Castle. The plaque is located at the entrance to the bridge crossing into the Castle from the Central Plaza. The elaborate "Time Castle" was reportedly dug up the day after it was buried and replaced with a more durable, plain container. The "Time Castle" was then said to have been taken to the Disney Archives. I have spoken with a former cast member who told me that as of last year, the capsule had never been brought to the archive and that this was probably an urban legend. (N: 87)

ABOVE: It is a Disneyland urban legend that this marker was placed on the exact center of Disneyland as it existed on opening day, July 17, 1955. This marker is not the center of Disneyland. This is a survey marker that was used in the initial construction of Disneyland. The survey marker was used to ensure proper alignment of Main Street U.S.A. and with both ends (Sleeping Beauty Castle and Main Street Station). The marker can be found after walking across the bridge and through the castle, then look down. (N:9) The center of Disneyland at the time of construction would have been closer to the Partners statue in the Central Plaza and a little north. (N: 86)

ABOVE AND BELOW: "Hand-rendered frescos" of scenes from *Sleeping Beauty*. These pictures are in the castle walkway between the Central Plaza and Fantasyland. They are located high on the walls, on the right and left sides just before you exit into Fantasyland, as you pass through on the walkway. (N: 92)

LEFT AND BELOW: Did you ever notice those squirrels on the sides of the castle? They are not just decorations; they are functioning storm drains for the castle. The drains were inspired by Sleeping Beauty's animal friends. (N:10)

LEFT: Guests approaching the castle see a frontal view of the squirrels and mistake them for gargoyles. This is the source of the belief that there are gargoyles on Sleeping Beauty Castle. (N: 11)

There are thirteen gargoyles on Cinderella's Castle at the Magic Kingdom in Walt Disney World. (N: 91)

ABOVE: You may have noticed a door at the back of the castle between the drinking fountain and the walkway to the Princess Fantasy Faire. It wasn't marked, and many people remember there being a tour through the castle. Many guests probably mistakenly took the door to be a service cast member door. The door is actually the entrance to the Sleeping Beauty Castle Walk-Through. This self guided tour consists of several dioramas and a few other surprises. The original tour was opened April 29, 1957, by former child star Shirley Temple Black. The attraction was closed on October 7, 2001. The Dioramas were refurbished and reopened November 2008, and is a walking tour of the story of Sleeping Beauty. It consists of several 3-D scenes of this wonderful story. There is a video display for guests who can't navigate the stairs.(N: 13)

ABOVE: Many people see the chandelier hanging on the back of the castle as you walk through to Fantasyland. But look again; it is actually a clock.

Side Note 1: There is an urban legend the time on the clock (12:23) honors the time of Walt Disney's passing. Walt actually passed away December 15, 1966 at 9:35 a.m...

Side Note 2: The clock is located on the back-side of the castle. The top of the castle façade was actually supposed to face the front? For aesthetic reasons, Walt decided to turn the castle around 180 degrees. I think he made the right choice. (N: 12)

LEFT AND BELOW: Not wanting to have just any run-of-the-mill water fountain at the beautiful Sleeping Beauty Castle, this fountain was installed at the back of the Castle. As you walk through the castle from Main Street, turn left. It has a wonderful statue of Aurora and Prince Phillip dancing. If you look very close, you may see one or more of the three fairies (Flora, Fauna, and Merryweather) flying behind Aurora and Prince Phillip.

Guest Information

Mickeys, Mickeys, Everywhere

Every Disney fan has probably heard the famous statement by Walt Disney that "...it was all started by a mouse." Mickey is the most popular character and can be seen everywhere. People even know there are Hidden Mickeys all over the park. But there are plenty of Mickeys that are in plain sight that most people never even notice. Here are a few:

ABOVE: Theatrical masks, Town Square, Main Street U.S.A. (behind Mad Hatter).

RIGHT: Back side of ticket turnstiles at the Park's Main Entrance.

PREVIOUS PAGE:

TOP: Guest Information area in front of Disneyland entrance.

MIDDLE: Balcony in New Orleans Square during the 50th anniversary.

BOTTOM LEFT: Tea Cups lights during the 50th anniversary.

BOTTOM RIGHT: Rockin' Both Parks sign in front of Harbor street side security check point.

ABOVE: Merchandise display in Tomorrowland's Star Trader store.

LEFT: Merchandise display in Tomorrowland's Tomorrowlanding hat store.

BELOW: Merchandise display window at the Tomorrowland's Star Trader store.

BELOW: The Honey, I Shrank the Audience announcement sign that the show can be heard in Spanish and Japanese.

BELOW: Even the food carts can't escape Mickey. This Mickey is located on the end of the handle used to control an ice cream delivery cartwhich was delivering stock to a vendor in front of the Mark Twain/Columbia loading area.

ABOVE: Road sign on Autopia.

ABOVE: High chairs are even getting into the act. These high chairs were located in front of the French Market in New Orleans Square.

LEFT AND BELOW: Christmas wreaths in Mickey's Toontown.

LEFT: Top of Christmas display for the Hannah Montana Christmas performance recorded at Disneyland in November 2008.

ABOVE Mickey on armor in Pirates of the Caribbean. In the scene just before you go back up the waterfall, look back over your left shoulder. This is actually a Hidden Mickey.

ABOVE: Bass drum in the Disneyland Marching Band on Main Street.

RIGHT: Splash Mountain just before the logs go back into the loading area. (NOTE: Guest blurred by author.)

And, of course, you would expect a lot of Mickeys in Mickey's and Minnie's houses located in Mickey's Toontown.

LEFT: Refrigerator magnet and picture on Minnie Mouse's refrigerator.

LEFT: : Welcome mat in front of Mickey's house.

ABOVE: Light in front yard of Mickey's house.

LEFT: Mickey's mailbox in front of Mickey's house .

ABOVE: Mickey Mouse's passport, located inside Mickey's house in the queue area. Notice the stamps. They are from Orlando, Tokyo, and Paris, the three park locations built after Disneyland. The dates are the opening dates of each resort. (N: 14)

BELOW: The music roll on Mickey's player piano.

ABOVE: City seal in Mickey's Toontown. The year is the date of Mickey's creation.

ABOVE: The answering machine in Minnie's house looks familiar.

BELOW: Meet Mickey sign in front of Mickey's house.

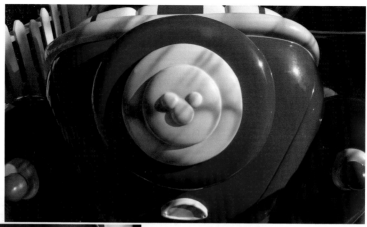

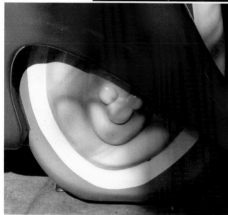

ABOVE AND LEFT: The car in front of the exit from Mickey's house (garage). The hubcaps and tire cover look familiar.

During the 50th anniversary of Disneyland, numerous Mickeys featuring the special "50" logo were added throughout the resort.

ABOVE: Meant to represent a Swiss canton. the crest hung over the entrance to the Matterhorn Bobsleds.

LEFT: A Mickey that at first glance looks like barrels in a cargo net. Located at entrance to Indiana Jones Fast Pass area.

Two of the my favorite Mickeys, which most people do actually see, but that I have to show anyway are...

ABOVE: Mickey Mouse flower portrait display inside thePark's main entrance. The basic shape of the Mickey head stays the same but seasonal and event changes are made to it regularly. The shape of his face, eyes, mouth, etc., are created by fiberglass header boards put into the ground. Gardeners then just place the perennials of different colors into each section. (N: 81)

BELOW LEFT: How the Mickey Mouse flower appeared for the "Celebrate" celebration in 2009.

BELOW RIGHT: How it appeared for the 50th anniversary celebration. Look closely and you can see the outside edge of the form for this face.

ABOVE: Walt and Mickey Partners Statue in Central Plaza in front of Sleeping Beauty Castle. A wonderful tribute and a great photo-opportunity location. There are reports that his ring is a Hidden Mickey. I had the opportunity to examine the ring close up at the Walt Disney Studios and it is not a Hidden Mickey.

LEFT: If you take a close look at Walt Disney's tie, you will see the stylized letters STR embroidered there. This represents the Smoke Tree Ranch in Palm Springs, California. It was one of Walt Disney's favorite vacation locations. He was often seen with these letters embroidered on his ties. (N: 15)

OK,
A Few Hidden
Mickeys

OK, for those of you who must see some "Hidden Mickeys", here are a few.

RIGHT: As you approach the second lift on the Big Thunder Mountain Railroad attraction, look to your left to see these gears in a familiar pattern.

LEFT: While in line for Big Thunder Mountain Railroad, as you pass under the train trestle, look at the rock wall to your right.

RIGHT: Is this a coincidence or does this cactus look strangely familiar? As you exit Big Thunder Mountain Railroad, look at the cactus to your right. Like most plants, this changes from time to time. Look around and you can usually find one.

BELOW and RIGHT: Could these be a Hidden Mickeys in the rock face of the walls for the line in the Finding Nemo Submarine attraction?

NOTE: Although the shapes are there, the author did darken the color of the shape so the reader could see them easier. I leave it up to the reader to decide if either of these are Hidden Mickeys.

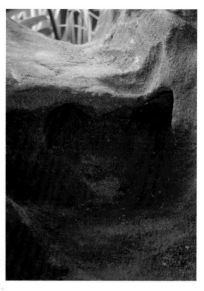

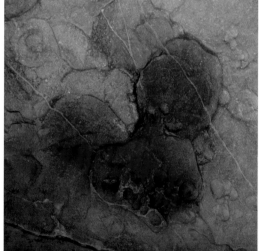

BELOW: Just before you enter the autograph area to Tinker Bell, look at the mushroom to the right.

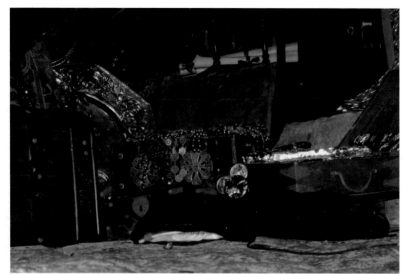

ABOVE: In the final Pirates of the Caribbean scene, where Jack is accepting his stipends, there are three coins that suspiciously look like a familiar mouse lying to the right, in front of treasure chests. See if you can find it next time you are on the attraction. This one is moved from time to time, so look for it carefully.

ABOVE AND RIGHT: Just after you enter the battle scene between the Wicked Wench and the fort, look to your right at the fort. You will notice holes in the wall that have been made by the cannonballs. In the center near the top, three cannonballs have left a familiar mouse.

LEFT: The barrels hanging over guests' heads just before going back up the waterfall in Pirates of the Caribbean.

RIGHT: Some people claim this as a Hidden Mickey; others say it is not. Not all Hidden Mickeys look like a perfect Mickey head. This one can be found as you exit the Pirates of the Caribbean attraction. Look at the first window to your right and you will see this lock being used to "secure" a window for the Pieces of Eight store.

I leave it up to the reader to decide if either of these are a Hidden Mickey.

BELOW: As you are waiting in the line above the Space Mountain loading area, look at the speakers in the guest rockets. They are going to rock your mouse.

ABOVE: Is it just me, or does the hole in the Matterhorn where the Skyway holes used to be, look a lot like a Mickey from this angle? Viewed from Innoventions it does not. I have viewed the Matterhorn from several different angles. Sometimes it does look like Mickey and others times it just looks like a hole. Don't worry; the recent plussing (DL) of the Matterhorn made it look great and did not change this feature.

NOTE: This image was not enhanced so that the Mickey would stand out. It is how it appears.

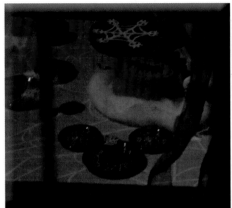

LEFT (2009) and BELOW (2010): In the banquet/dance scene in the Haunted Mansion, look at the place settings. The plates at one setting should look familiar. Although usually done with white plates, during the holiday season, when Jack takes over, the plates turn to a more Halloween mood. They occasionally move the setting, so you may have to look around the table to find it.

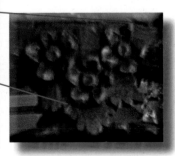

ABOVE: When you first enter the Haunted Mansion, look on the wall to the right. At the top of the mirror, you will see a traditional Hidden Mickey made of flowers.

RIGHT: On the Splash Mountain attraction, just before you return to the loading/unloading area, look to your left. You may have to look back slightly.

LEFT: After you enter the indoor portion of the Buzz Lightyear queue, look at the maps straight ahead on the wall. The planet in Sector 1 looks like a great place to vacation.

RIGHT: Could this be a hidden Wall-E? This montage can be found in the Big Thunder Mountain Railroad queue, just in front of the mule engine.

"I'm Not Bad, I'm Just Drawn That Way..."

Although The Walt Disney Company in general, and Disneyland specifically, is a very clean and wholesome, family-orientated organization, sometimes they can get a little "bad." Here are a few pictures that I'm sure millions of people have seen, but have never really seen. This first two pages consist of various scenes from the Pirates of the Caribbean.

LEFT: The Auction: "Take A Wench For A Bride" - "We wants the Redhead!"

BELOW: "A Portrait of Things to Come" in the Pirates' Tavern. The painting is reportedly the "Redhead" after being bought and turned into a pirate wench. (N: 104)

ABOVE: In the original cantina scene, most of the women were being chased by the pirates. Today, only this one is still chasing a female, and he is after her "food." (N: 17)

LEFT AND RIGHT: Two paintings in the queue just inside the entrance to the Pirates of the Caribbean.

The picture on the right is of a park guest who won a contest. She has a wonderful rose in her mouth. This picture has since been removed. (N: 16)

The picture on the left is of two famous female pirates.

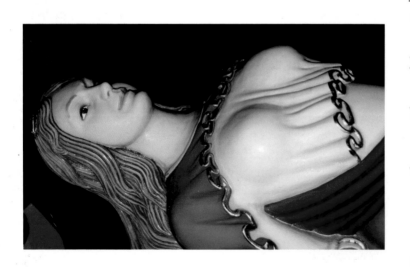

Have you seen these maidens of the sea?   This romantic figurehead can be found on the bow of the Sailing Ship Columbia. Her hair and dress are gracefully flowing with the wind.

This figurehead is mounted on the building at Lafitte's Tavern (formerly Harper's Mill), on Tom Sawyer Island/ Pirates' Lair. This beauty graces the outside of the tavern enticing pirates to drop some pieces of eight in return for a refreshing beverage.

Disney's most famous bad girl, and my personal favorite, Jessica Rabbit.

ABOVE: Jessica about to teach a weasel a lesson in the Roger Rabbit attraction.

ABOVE: The entrance to the women's bathroom in Mickey's Toontown Garage.

BELOW: Jessica's mailbox in the Mickey's Toontown Post Office.

BELOW: How did she get into the Roger Rabbit attraction?

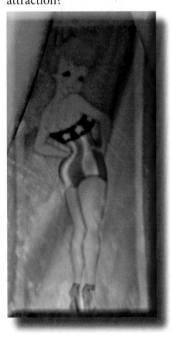

LEFT: Silhouette of Jessica Rabbit walking back and forth in the Roger Rabbit queue.

RIGHT: A magazine left on the arm of one of Minnie Mouse's chairs.

Actually, she's not bad, she's just drawn that way....

Watch Your Step!

The ground in Disneyland is not just paved or paved and painted. Thought is given to the theme of the area and the ground is decorated to enhance the theme. Where bricks are used, they're not just laid out in a typical box design, but are made into geometric designs. Even the feel changes from land to land to give guests a tactile sense of the change. (N: 19)

LEFT: This Disneyland manhole cover is located on the sidewalk in front of the Emporium, Main Street U.S.A. . It is on the corner closest to the Town Square.

RIGHT: Manhole or Mousehole cover in Mickey's Toontown, located near the fountain. You might be surprised what happens when you step on the one by the Toontown Five & Dime store.

LEFT: Welcome mat in front of Minnie Mouse's house. Quiz: What is Minnie Mouse's real first name?
(See note N: 18 for answer.)

LEFT: A wooden plank walkway from the Fantasy Faire to Rancho del Zocalo restaurant.

RIGHT: Faux wooden 4x4 in Critter Country.

LEFT: Intricate brick work in Tomorrowland.

RIGHT: Cobblestone street in Fantasyland. Fortunately for guests, the surface is not real cobblestone, otherwise guests would be tripping all over the place.

During the construction of Disneyland, as with any major construction project, surveys were taken and markers put down to ensure proper position and alignment. One of the original survey markers can be seen in the chapter on Sleeping Beauty Castle. The survey markers were left to give remodeling crews permanent fixed reference points. Here are four more that were added during subsequent remodels.

LEFT: This marker is located in Frontierland, just to the left of the Mark Twain/Columbia dock.

RIGHT: This marker is located in front of and to the far right of the entrance to the Pirates of the Caribbean.

LEFT: This marker is located in the intersection between the Matterhorn, Tomorrowland Terrace, and Finding Nemo Submarines.

RIGHT: This marker is in intersection of the Matterhorn, Sleeping Beauty Castle, and Tinker Bell's Pixie Hollow autograph area.

LEFT AND BELOW:
Horseshoe and wagon
tracks left in the faux dirt in
Frontierland.

BELOW: Cowboy boots
track left in the faux dirt in
Frontierland.

RIGHT: A small cover I noticed on the
walkway between the Central Plaza and
the Astro Orbitor. At first I thought it was
strange to see "WDW", which normally,
represents Walt Disney World, at
Disneyland. It's been pointed out to me
that this could refer to "Walt Disney
Water", but that is speculation. Or could
it all just be a coincidence?

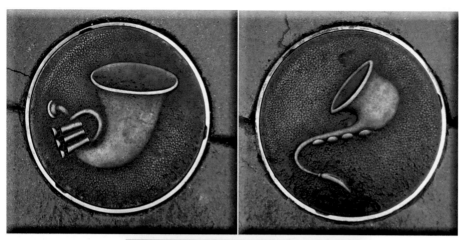

THIS PAGE: Have you ever noticed the fountain in front of Mickey's house in Toontown? You're saying we got you this time. For some reason he has a music director's baton. Well, look down at the ground as you walk around the fountain, and you'll see his orchestra.

You really have to watch your step with these four horns. Go ahead, step on one. Is that a horn you hear coming from the fountain?

ABOVE: The tile walkway in what was formerly the Aladdin & Jasmine's Story Tale Adventures in Aladdin's Oasis, looks like a magic carpet.

ABOVE: The brick work can be found all the way around the Central Plaza. This design is not just rectangle bricks laid side-by-side. A beautiful pattern is done.

Signs
Or,
What Did
That Say?

CAUTION
GAGS
AHEAD

WRONG TURN O.K.

As you would expect with anything in Mickey's Toontown, the signs are not your ordinary signs.

CHAPTER TITLE PAGE: Both of these street signs can be found in Mickey's Toontown.

BELOW: Dalmatians are a traditional fire station dog. In Toontown, the 101st Engine Company has the 101 Dalmatians as their mascots..

LEFT: The official seal of Mickey's Toontown literally is a seal.

BELOW: And Roger Rabbit is on the one zillion dollar, ahh, one zillion simoleon bill.

RIGHT: Nothing like sure directions when it comes to electricity. You might find the results shocking!

By Order of the
TOONTOWN POWER COMPANY

OPENING THIS DOOR IS
ABSOLUTELY POSITIVELY
and UNQUESTIONABLY
FORBIDDEN!

Unless you really
feel like it

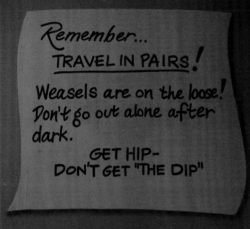

Remember...
TRAVEL IN PAIRS!

Weasels are on the loose!
Don't go out alone after dark.

GET HIP-
DON'T GET "THE DIP"

LEFT: A "cool" warning from the "hip" crowd.

BELOW LEFT AND BELOW RIGHT: Personalized Mickey's Toontown license plates mounted just inside the entrance to Roger Rabbit's Car Toon Spin (enter then look back at the wall). Can you read them? (See note N: 20 for answers.)

74

ABOVE: In Fantasyland, you had better watch out for the Mad Hatter. Now which way is that Tea Party? I wouldn't want to be late!

BELOW: Now look who has been put in charge of safety. Oh my!

FOR YOUR SAFETY

REMAIN SEATED WITH HANDS, ARMS, FEET AND LEGS INSIDE THE VEHICLE.

SUPERVISE CHILDREN.

TOP: At the new (2010) entrance to Mickey's Toontown is the town's welcome sign.

BELOW: The original entrance sign that kept, ahh, count of the residents.

BELOW: As with any town, Mickey's Toontown has its share of local clubs and fraternal organizations. Here are a few examples. They are all familiar but not quite what they first appear to be.

ABOVE: Another zany Toontown traffic sign. Which way do I go?

ABOVE: In the case of this Toontown sign, you better really watch out for a fork in the road. Not really, but you better always be safe than sorry with signs in Mickey's Toontown.

BOTTOM LEFT: Are they talking about the guests, cast members, Goofy, or a real chicken crossing the road?

BOTTOM RIGHT: This is actually a real sign, but done in Disneyland's playful way.

ABOVE: Toons are always dropping safes on peoples' heads. Well, that's what they say in the movie.

RIGHT: This Autopia sign shows you the driving conditions you can expect.

LEFT: This Autopia sign reminds everyone who helped start Disneyland, and you better watch out for him.

BELOW: I'm always looking for something gnu, I mean new, at Disneyland.

ABOVE: This Autopia sign is not just a tribute to the famous Route 66. It is also a tribute to the opening year of Disneyland.

As Seen In The Movies

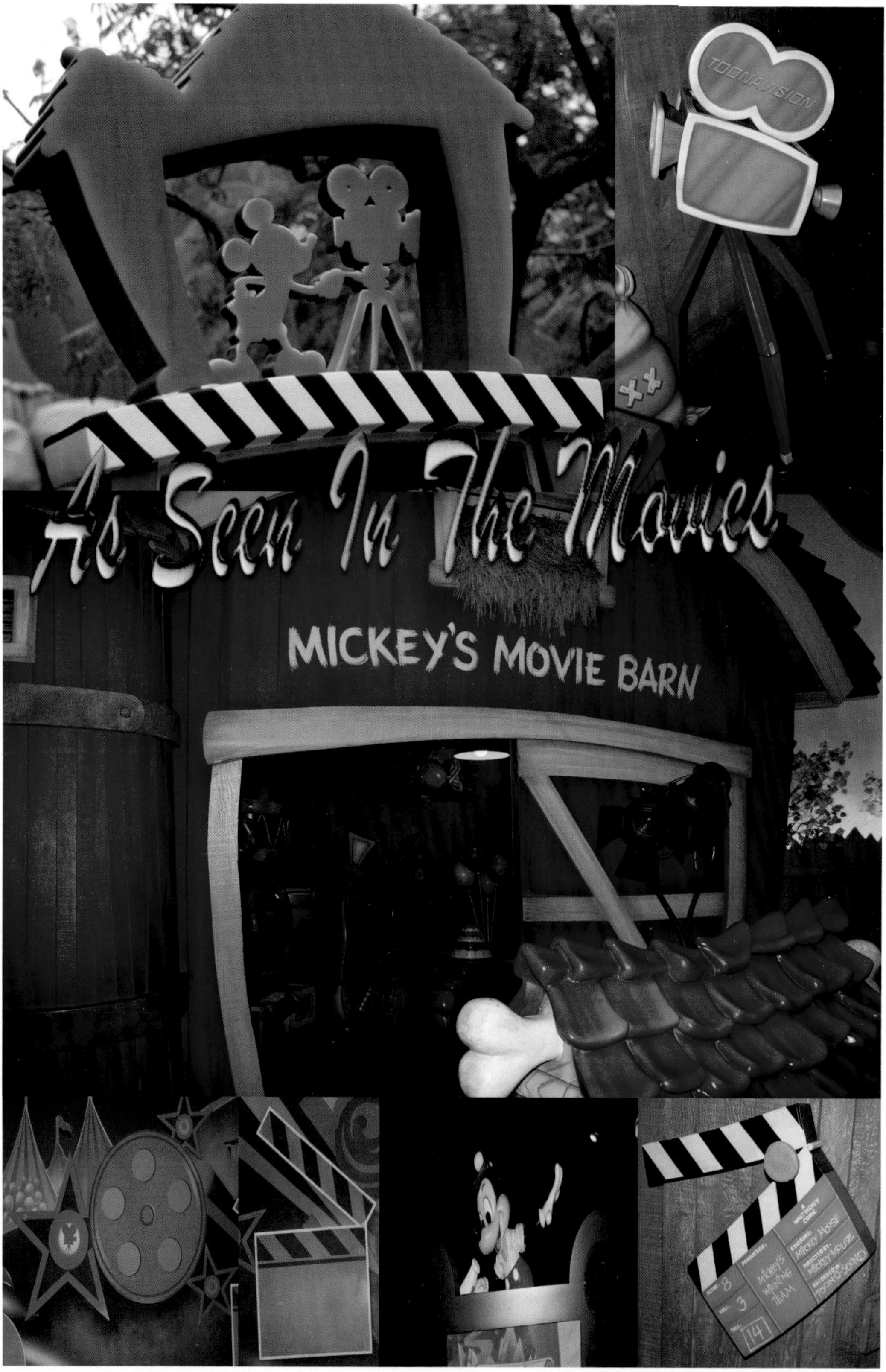

MICKEY'S MOVIE BARN

Disneyland uses many props for the themes in the various attractions. Many are familiar re-creations of famous movie props. Are you aware that many of those props are actually from the movies they represent? The R2-D2 and C-3PO droids inside the main entrance to Star Tours were actually used in the original Star Wars movies.

ABOVE AND TOP FOLLOWING PAGE: The two lovable droids from Star Wars. C-3PO is actually plated with real gold leaf. This not only gave George Lucas the look he wanted, but it also prevented oxidation while filming in the desert. (N: 21)

PREVIOUS PAGE: Sign in front of Mickey's house (top left), camera inside Mickey's house (top right), Mickey's Movie Barn inside Mickey's house (middle), clapper boards in Mickey's house (bottom right), Mickey inside Innoventions (bottom second from right), and miscellaneous pictures from Innoventions (bottom left two).

During the 2011 reimagineering (DL) of Star Tours, Imagineers gave R2-D2 a slightly newer, no older, Starspeeder 1000 than the damaged one he is shown in below.

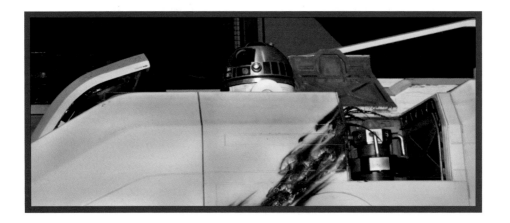

ABOVE: The original Starspeeder 3000.

ABOVE: Starspeeder 1000 after the 2011 reimagineering.

ABOVE : The ore car used in *Indiana Jones and the Temple of Doom.* (N: 22)

LEFT: The bars mounted on the sides of the front bumper were to assist the stunt man in climbing and holding on during the scene. Golf balls were mounted on top of bars to keep their hands from slipping off.

BELOW: The German truck used in the chase scene from *Indiana Jones and the Raiders of the Lost Ark.*

For Disney movie fans, you may remember the comedy classic *Hot Lead & Cold Feet*. The movie had many wonderful stars including the great Don Knotts as the Denver Kid and Jim Dale as twin brothers Eli and Wild Billy (also Jasper Bloodshy). The brothers get into a competition that ends in a race on two small trains (Iron Donkeys or Mull Engines). Those trains are now props at Big Thunder Mountain Railroad. A person with a sharp eye will note that both trains are now marked II. This is in honor of the winning engine. Do you know which engine won? (See note N: 23 for answer.)

ABOVE: Located in the queue to Big Thunder Mountain Railroad, just past the point where you pass under the train trestle. It is on your right.

BELOW: Located at the back of Big Thunder Mountain Railroad, on the walkway between Frontierland and Fantasyland.

ABOVE AND FOLLOWING PAGE: The Disneyland New Orleans Train Station was originally located on the opposite side of the tracks. During the Park expansion that included the addition of the Pirates of the Caribbean and Haunted Mansion attractions, the station was moved across the tracks and turned 180 degrees due to room constraints. If the station looks familiar, that is because the building is an exact replica of the station used in the 1949 Disney movie, *So Dear To My Heart*. (N:24)

If you listen carefully while waiting at the station, you will hear the classic clicking noise of a telegraph operator. For those trained in Continental Code (not the more familiar Morse Code), the message is the opening day speech given by Walt Disney on the day Disneyland first opened on July 17, 1955. The clicking noises were corrupted at some point after installation, most likely during a hardware update. The error was eventually caught by a sharp guest and the sound track corrected. (N: 82)

RIGHT: The Toontown Train Station is a caricature of the New Orleans Train Station. (N:105)

ABOVE: I had the good fortune of being delayed by "playful spooks" in my Doom Buggy one trip. I quickly sat my camera on the edge of the Doom Buggy and took this time-lapsed picture. I didn't want to scare the ghosts or ruin the experience for other guests, so I did not use a flash. Many people have seen Disney's epic *20,000 Leagues Under the Sea*. In the movie, Captain Nemo plays an organ. Shortly after filming was completed, Disney moved many of the props, including the organ, to a display in Tomorrowland. When they decided to remove that display, Disney Imagineers decided to use the organ as a prop in the then-new Haunted Mansion. This is Captain Nemo's original organ used in the movie. (N: 25)

Haven't I Seen That Before?
Haven't I Seen That Before?

Some of you may have looked at props around the park and not realized that you had seen them before at other attractions. The most famous are the characters from America Sings. Most of the characters from this attraction were re-used in the construction of Splash Mountain, although a couple stopped at Star Tours.

ABOVE: The guys can be seen in the first inside show area just after making the first hard left.

BELOW: These three characters are to the left after entering the grand finale section.

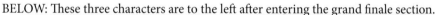

RIGHT: These two are just before you go up to the top of Chickapin Hill to take the big plunge. In America Sings, they told the story of Billy the Kid.

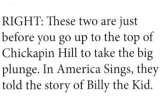

LEFT: These three baby opossums are just before you see the rabbit on the handcar.

ABOVE: This guy can be seen in the first show area just after making the first hard left.

LEFT: These two are just after the grand finale on the right. Br'er Fox was on the handcar in America Sings.

90

ABOVE: The grand finale of Splash Mountain. The name of the ship ZIP-A-DEE-Lady was added, but this is very similar to its appearance in America Sings.(N: 26)

RIGHT: Blue Bird of Happiness in the Finale.

BELOW: Just after you enter the cave for the grand finale, you can see these two pair of "love birds" on the right. In America Sings, they were in an old jalopy.

Prior to the installation of Star Tours, this space was home to Adventures Thru Inner Space, an attraction that took guests on a ride in an Atomobile. The guests were shrunk down using the "Mighty Microscope" and shown the inner working of a snowflake. Many "tributes" (DL) were included in the Star Tours attraction. After your Starspeeder takes off, Rex goes the wrong way to exit the facility and ends up in a repair bay. Just after he enters the bay and turns right, the nose of the Starspeeder is pointed down. If you look quickly to the right, mixed in with the equipment, you can clearly see the "Mighty Microscope." In Star Tours II, it can now be seen inside the Death Star. In the second section of the main queue, there were baskets moving overhead. One of the baskets carried an Atomobiles. The baskets were removed as part of the plussing. Watch the luggage security screen now for many wonderful tributes to various Disney and Lucas properties. (N: 28 /112)

BELOW: In the queue of Adventure Thru Inner Space, there were display consoles mounted that had various notices on them. One of the consoles could be seen as a repair console in the G2 droid area. The console was all the way down at the bottom of the repair area with an R4 unit in front of it. I have looked for the console since the 2011 plussing, but can't find the console. I spoke with a Disney Imagineer who told me they are pretty sure the console was removed, but keep trying to see it. You never know, it may come back. (N: 29)

As mentioned earlier, after America Sings was removed, many of the characters made their way to the new Splash Mountain. Two geese however, stopped off at Star Tours and never left. They became the G2 repair droids located in the queue. If you look closely at their feet, you can see they are webbed. (N: 27)

LEFT: As they appeared in the original Star Tours.

BELOW LEFT: During the 2011 reimagineering, the queue area was plussed to give it a cleaner transport terminal look. The repair droids were now given the jobs of security. The droid that used to fix other droids, is now responsible for screening your luggage. He was "cleaned up" and given a nice blue uniform shirt and shoes. You can still see those webbed feet.

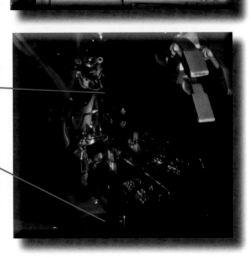

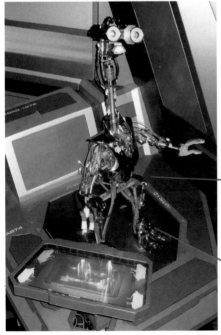

During the removal of Mine Train Through Nature's Wonderland, several parts were preserved and installed in the new Big Thunder Mountain Railroad or the surrounding area.

ABOVE: The original town from Mine Train Through Nature's Wonderland was moved to its new location as part of the queue and loading area for Big Thunder Mountain Railroad. This town is known as Rainbow Ridge. The town was renovated during the 2013 upgrade of Big Thunder Mountain Railroad. Do you know the population? (See note N: 35 for answer.)

BELOW: These dinosaur bones are at the end of the Big Thunder Mountain Railroad attraction. All of these props were part of Mine Train Through Nature's Wonderland except the rib bones above the riders' heads. These were added for the attraction. This area is called Dinosaur Gap. (N: 34/78)

ABOVE: The last of the original locomotives could be seen along the banks of Rivers of America. It was viewable from the Mark Twain/Columbia or from Tom Sawyer Island/Pirates' Lair. This is also the last piece of track left. Sadly guests can no longer see the train as it was removed during the 2010 refurbishment of the Rivers of America and is now at the Walt Disney Archives. (N: 30 /31 /79)

BELOW: The Prairie Dogs that inhabited the mine train were original characters from the Mine Train Through Nature's Wonderland. Sadly, most of the old characters were reportedly buried after removal and Big Thunder Mountain Railroad was built on top. (N: 32/33)

If you walk from Frontierland to Fantasyland on the path that takes you behind Big Thunder Mountain Railroad, you cross over a bridge that has a pond on the opposite side from Big Thunder Mountain Railroad. There you will see the following left over from the mine train attraction.

RIGHT: The tunnel that lead the train out over the water. This can be seen in some of the famous shots of the old train.

BELOW: The tunnel that led out to where the train sits along the Rivers of America (see prior page).

ABOVE: As you stand and look at the pond, you may notice an occasional splash. This is caused by the jumping fish that used to be a part of the mine train attraction. (N: 36)

ABOVE: If you've ever ridden the Mark Twain or Columbia, you've probably noticed the Indian Village at the back of Rivers of America. However, did you know that many parts of the settlement are from the actual original Indian village from opening day? The Indian Village was originally located in the area approximately to the right of the Pirates of the Caribbean entrance and toward the water. Back then, it had live Indian Cast members performing traditional dances and archery exhibition. The Indian Village was moved within a year towards what is now the entrance to Critter Country. The Indian War Canoes were added along with a Indian Trading Post store. In October 1971, the Indian Village was removed to make way for the new Bear Country. (N: 42)

LEFT: During the remodel of the Swiss Family Treehouse into Tarzan's Treehouse, the entire tree was stripped down and redone. This branch was redone and the "mind thy head" painted on it was not only as a warning, but an homage to the Swiss Family Treehouse. (N: 49)

In addition, the tree that Tarzan's Treehouse is located in is a special "Disney species." It is called Disneyodendron Semperflorens Grandis, which is "Latin" for large, ever blooming Disney tree. (N: 85)

ABOVE: There used to be five attractions on the Rivers of America: the Mark Twain, Columbia Sailing Ship, Indian War Canoes, Tom Sawyer Island Rafts, and Mike Fink Keel Boats. The Keel Boats originated on an episode of the Davy Crockett TV series. The boats used in the show were the original attraction's two boats. The boats were replaced by look-a-like ones made of fiberglass and were slightly larger. The boats loaded to the left of the Tom Sawyer rafts. They took a leisurely trip around Tom Sawyer Island. After this attraction closed, the Bertha Mae was sold but the Gullywhumper remained as a prop and tribute to the past. It was re-located to the back of the island. (N: 38)

BELOW: During the 2010 renovation of the Rivers of America, the Gullywhumper was removed and taken to the Disney Archives for preservation. After years of exposure to the elements, it was in bad shape. A new Gullywhumper was built and placed in front of the cabin, now themed to be Mike Fink's cabin. The new boat was built like the ones used in the original TV series.

Many people believe the present rocket attraction, the Astro Orbitor, is the original one just refurbished. Actually, it is not. The original rocket attraction has been converted and still sits atop the old People Mover station. It is now the Observatron, which activates every quarter hour.

Can you give all the names the rocket attraction has used?. (N: 84)

Can you name the twelve original Astro Jets? (N: 96)

ABOVE: is how it looked during the 50th celebration. To the right is how it normally appears.

The Autopia attraction is one of the most popular attractions at Disneyland and has existed in one form or another since the Park first opened. At one point in time, there were two Autopia attractions with two tracks each. One was in Fantasyland and loaded underneath the Monorail just to the left of the Bobsled entrance. The other was in Tomorrowland, approximately where it is today. In its present form, you ride on one of four tracks. The Car Park section of the Autopia attraction has two tributes. One to a current attraction (pictured below), and one to a former attraction (pictured next page) at Disneyland.

BELOW: One of the original Mr. Toad cars, which has been bronzed. The sign states this is a two seater car used from 1955 to 1996. (N: 80)

ABOVE: One of the original Midget Autopia cars. The sign says it was used in Fantasyland from 1956 to 1965. The car has been bronzed and is on loan from Marceline, Missouri. (N: 40)

Walt Disney was born in Chicago, IL. At age four, his family moved to the rural farming community of Marceline, where he lived until age nine. Disney considered Marceline his home town. Country life in Marceline fostered Disney's love of animals and wildlife, and his experiences there became the genesis of many of his ideas later in life. Marceline was also where Disney became interested in art, once painting the side of the family home with brushes dipped in tar. (N: 41)

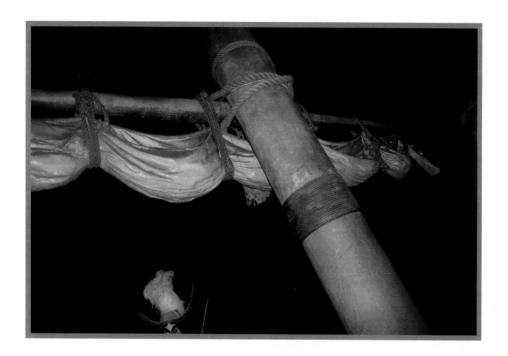

ABOVE AND BELOW: The rigging on the pirate's ship in Peter Pan was originally used on the pirates ship that was in the Skull Lagoon. The original ship was a restaurant sponsored by Chicken of the Sea (N: 44)

LEFT: When Pirates of the Caribbean first opened, there was a pirate-themed game arcade at the exit. This fortune telling pirate machine was part of that attraction. It is now located in the breezeway between the Pieces of Eight store and Le Bat en Rouge store. (N: 45)

RIGHT: The map the pirate points to is original artwork. The map was created by an Imagineer named Sam McKim. He created a lot of the concept art for many of the more popular Disneyland attractions including Pirates of the Caribbean, Carousel of Progress, Great Moments with Mr. Lincoln, and the Haunted Mansion. Probably his best-known works are the souvenir Disneyland wall maps. (N: 83)

Back when Critter Country was Bear Country, the main attraction was the Country Bear Jamboree. Anyone who went to this attraction remembers the heckler animal heads hanging on the wall (Max, Buff, and Melvin). The show was very popular, but sadly was eventually closed and moved the parts moved to to Walt Disney World to be used in thier attraction. The three hecklers however decided to stay and hide in the new Adventures with Winnie the Pooh attraction. The Country Bear Jamboree is still playing at The Magic Kingdom in Walt Disney World.

RIGHT: Speaking of Winnie the Pooh, if his honey pot balloon looks familiar, it was originally the swing that Teddy Barra lowered from the ceiling in the original show. She was the last of the big-time swingers. (N: 43)

BELOW: Just after the scene where Pooh is floating in the Honey Pot Balloon, you enter a new area. Look back and up to see these rascals still at Disneyland. (N: 77)

LEFT AND BELOW: Many people think these are just clever display cases in the Little Green Men Store Command. They are actually rocket ships from the original rocket attraction. These rockets used to be attached to the Observatron's arms. (N: 46)

BELOW: These are reportedly the doors from one of the original People Mover cars. They appear to be replicas, but an Imagineer I spoke with said they are real. They are now used as decoration/theme for the counter in the Little Green Men Store Command. (N: 47)

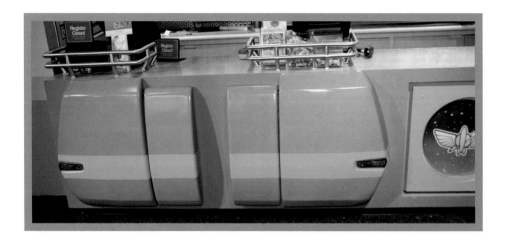

BELOW: Most people who have been to Disneyland are familiar with the Disneyland Railroad Tomorrowland Station. What most people don't know is that this station used to be the loading station for the old Viewliner train attraction. The Viewliner opened June 26, 1957, and was located approximately where the Finding Nemo Submarine attraction is now. The attraction was one of the shortest-lived attractions, closing September 15, 1958. Two of the trains that this station now services are original Disneyland attractions. (N: 48)

I WANT SOME POPCORN

POPCORN

One of the most popular snacks at Disneyland is popcorn. Guests consume 43.7 million boxes of popcorn every year, so there should be no surprise that Disneyland would not simply have a standard popcorn cart. Not only are their popcorn carts efficiently producing a steady stream of the snack, they are themed to match the area, or at least to Disney. Each cart has a little character called a "Roastie-Toastie" that rotates the drums of popcorn. These carts can be seen throughout the park. (N: 50/51)

BELOW: This Dapper Dan is located in the Town Square in front of City Hall. (NOTE: The Roastie-Toasties are moved around. Just look around and you will find them.)

BELOW: This Dapper Dan is located in Frontierland to the left of the Mark Twain/ Columbia dock area.

ABOVE: The Abominable Snow Man can be seen in the popcorn machine in front of the Fantasyland gift shop near the Matterhorn exit.

ABOVE: The Rocketeer can be seen in Tomorrowland by the old People Mover/rocket attraction platforms.

ABOVE: This little clown is located in Fantasyland next to It's a Small World.

LEFT: In the Central Plaza in front of the "Partners" Statue, you will find this clown, but during the holiday season, he is replaced with Santa Claus (see next page).

RIGHT: This little guy can be seen in Mickey's Toontown at the exit to Mickey's house.

LEFT: During the holiday season, the Haunted Mansion is given a makeover, transforming the attraction into its "Nightmare Before Christmas" theme. The popcorn machine is changed to have the Oogie Boogie Man. He can also be seen inside the attraction.

RIGHT: During the rest of the year, this ghoul can be seen in New Orleans Square just outside the Haunted Mansion.

LEFT: In the Central Plaza in Front of the "Partners" Statue, you will find Santa Claus during the holiday season.

RESTROOMS

Since starting this book, I have been looking for things I've never noticed before. While sitting outside the Autopia restrooms waiting for my family, I noticed that they were not marked with the traditional "MEN," "WOMEN," or even a simple circle and triangle. They were marked with "alien" looking creatures consistent with being in Tomorrowland. I began wondering what other signs had been used at the other bathrooms around the park I had seen hundreds of times, but never had really seen.

Tomorrowland

ABOVE AND RIGHT: The Men's and Women's restroom signs between Autopia and Carousel of Progress.

PREVIOUS PAGE: This Cheshire cat can be seen to the right of the restrooms in Sleeping Beauty castle.

ABOVE AND RIGHT: Space Mountain. Same signs with the Men and Women added below.

Frontierland

ABOVE AND RIGHT: Restrooms next to the entrance to Rancho del Zocalo Restaurante. They are in the breezeway between the Restaurante and the Fantasy Faire princess meet and greet area (formerly Plaza Gardens Stage).

Fantasyland

LEFT AND BELOW: Restrooms in Sleeping Beauty Castle, next to Alice in Wonderland. The restrooms are located on the path between the castle and the Matterhorn. The character signs represent the King and Queen of Hearts from the *Alice in Wonderland* movie.

LEFT AND BELOW: Restrooms at the entrance to Fantasyland Theater (formerly the Princess Fantasy Faire).

THIS PAGE: Restrooms at the Village Haus Restaurant. Located to the right of the restaurant entrance, on the path to Frontierland. The marionettes pay homage to *Pinocchio*.

Adventureland

THIS PAGE: These restrooms signs are located at the intersection between the Tiki Room, Pioneer Mercantile, and South Seas Traders.

Critter Country

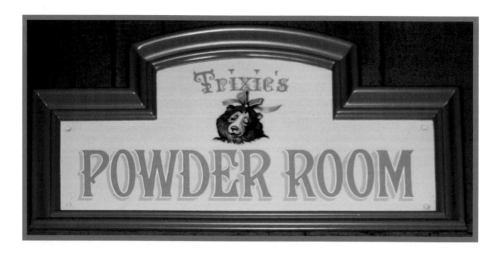

ABOVE AND BELOW: The Critter Country restrooms, errrrr, Gentlemen's Lair and Powder Rooms, are located on the lower level of the Hungry Bear Restaurant. The signs are reminiscent of the days when the land was called Bear Country, and the main attraction was the Country Bear Jamboree. Gomer and Trixie were characters in the show.

Tom Sawyer Island/Pirates' Lair

ABOVE AND BELOW RIGHT: There are two sets of restrooms on Tom Sawyer Island/Pirates' Lair. One set is located at Fort Wilderness. When facing the front gates of the fort, they are to the right. These pictures were taken at that set of restrooms at Fort Wilderness. There is a male, a female and a family restroom.

The second set is located on the opposite end of the island near the water wheel. They have the same door logos but only have a male and female set of restrooms.

BELOW LEFT: Sign at restrooms near water wheel explaining how to get to Fort Wilderness restrooms.

Mickey's Toontown

ABOVE AND BELOW: These restrooms are located in Mickey's Toontown, at the gas station. They are themed for the Roger Rabbit attraction.

New Orleans Square

These restrooms are located in New Orleans Square. They are behind the New Orleans Pin Trading store, and just to the left of the New Orleans Disneyland Train Station.

Main Street
U.S.A.

These restroom signs on Main Street U.S.A. are themed to the turn-of-the-century, any-town main street.

ABOVE: These restrooms are located at City Hall, to the right of the front doors.

BELOW: These restrooms are located between the Plaza Inn restaurant and Star Tours. They are technically listed as Tomorrowland restrooms, although they have the Main Street Theme.

For many years this restroom was listed on the Disneyland maps that everyone could pick up when entering the park. Then suddenly, Disneyland stopped listing it. The restroom was eventually listed again on the Park maps, but it was listed as a family restroom. It was not located in an obvious location and was easily overlooked. I was unaware of this restroom until reading about it on a web page as part of my research for this book. The restroom was especially spacious and perfect for family use. Disneyland has never tried to hide the restroom and openly told guests of its existence, especially families and guests with disabilities. But that did not stop it from becoming a Disneyland urban legend. The restroom became known as the "secret restroom." The restroom was removed in 2013 as part of a major new addition to the Park. Can you guess where this restroom was located? I'll give you a hint: look at the door logo to get you started. (N: 52)

LEFT: Full view of the door.

RIGHT: The family bathroom logo on the door.

As an added quiz, there are 25 sets of restrooms open to the public in Disneyland. Can you name their locations? (See note N: 113 for answers.)

DISNEYLAND
DOORS

Knock, Knock. Oh, Mr. White Rabbit?

Most people have heard of the windows on Main Street U.S.A. and other locations throughout the park. Some are just humorous windows, but most pay tribute to important people in the Disney organization. There are many great books that you can read abut these tributes, so I decided

to look at the doors. Anytime you enter a Disneyland building, you go through a door. There are also doors you don't go through. Many of these doors have something special about them. Here are just a few.

LEFT: This door is part of Sleeping Beauty Castle. Located on the Fantasyland side to the left of the tunnel that leads to the Snow White Grotto. At first glance the door just looks like any other with a lot of ornate metal work. If you look closer, you'll see it actually looks like a dragon, or could it just be a lizard?

BELOW AND RIGHT: Toontown Power Company door. You might get a real shock opening this one.

By Order of the
TOONTOWN POWER COMPANY

OPENING THIS DOOR IS
ABSOLUTELY, POSITIVELY
and UNQUESTIONABLY
FORBIDDEN!

Unless you really
feel like it

All of these doors are in Toontown.

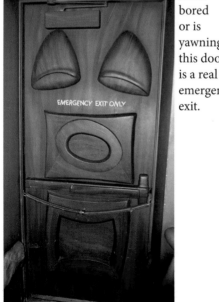

> We Cover Toons For
> Any Permanent Injury Caused
> By:
>
> Hotfoots
> X
> Explosions
> X
> Falling Off Cliffs
> X
> TNT Disguised As Cigars
> X
> Getting Hit On The Head
> X
> Booby Trapped Gift Boxes
> X
> Falling Anvils-Safes-Pianos
> X
> Getting Run Over By Steamrollers
> X
> Smashing Into Brick Walls
> Disguised As Tunnels
>
> Any Other Animated Adversities
> Not Listed Herewith

ABOVE AND ABOVE LEFT:The local insurance company that covers everything a toon needs. Unfortunately, they are out of business.

BELOW RIGHT: Jessica Rabbit's dressing room.

BELOW LEFT: Emergency exit door in Roger Rabbit. In spite of the fact the door looks bored or is yawning, this door is a real emergency exit.

Thousands of guests pass this door each year while walking in New Orleans Square and never realize what's on the other side. Club 33 is located above the Blue Bayou restaurant. To access the club, guests enter this door and either go up some stairs or take a small elevator to the second floor. Club 33 was originally designed to be a private location Walt Disney could take special guests to have a private dinner. Membership is now open to all guests but is limited. The waiting list was reported to be in excess of 14 years. With the addition of 1901 club this number will go up. Club 33 has both private and business memberships. A major renovation of Club 33 will take place in 2014. When completed, this door will no longer be the main entrance. The new doorway will be where the L 'Ornement Magique store is and the Court de Anges (Court of Angels) will act as the waiting / entrance area. The door is reportedly going to remain as a tribute to the former entrance. (N: 54)

BELOW: Probably Disneyland's most famous door. Very few guests get to pass through the door into Club 33. The door is located to the right of the entrance to the Blue Bayou restaurant in New Orleans Square.

ABOVE: Inside the alcove and to the left is the intercom system used to gain access to Club 33.

Gone, but Still There

Or, the Ghosts of Disneyland Attractions Past

When Mickey's Toontown first opened, the land had an attraction called the Jolly Trolley, which traveled from one end of Toontown and back. The distance was short, the lines were long, and during the busy seasons the trolley could barely move. The attraction eventually closed, but the track was left in place. Recently, one of the trolleys has reappeared as a static attraction and makes for a great photo opportunity.

BELOW: One of the original Jolly Trolleys. You can find the trolley just after you enter Mickey's Toontown. It is the older cousin to the current Red Car Trolleys in Disney California Adventure.

RIGHT: The Jolly Trolley house, located to the right of Roger Rabbit.

One of the original Mickey's Toontown attractions was The Acorn Crawl, a ball pit located between Chip and Dale's Tree house and the exit from Mickey's house. This attraction was popular with the little ones. Slow ridership and hygiene issues eventually lead to the pits removal. (N: 55)

ABOVE: The Acorn Crawl as it appears today.

BELOW: This pit was filled with hundreds of plastic colored balls.

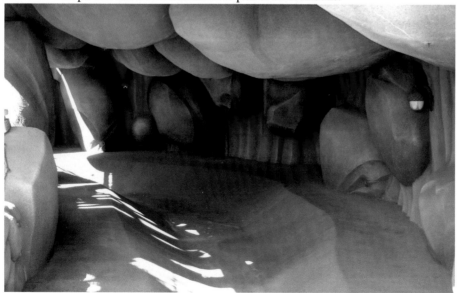

An extremely popular attraction in its day was the Skyway to Tomorrowland and the return trip the Skyway to Fantasyland. Originally, this was a round-trip attraction but it quickly became a one-way attraction. This attraction took guests in a small gondola from one land, high over the Park, to the other. Walt Disney never liked the large pylon holding the attraction next to his beautiful castle. When the Matterhorn was built, the pylon was hidden inside, which made for a ride through the mountain. Eventually, problems with riders, trouble with weather, a major necessary overhaul, and the addition of Indiana Jones attraction all led to the Skyway's demise. (N: 56)

ABOVE: The Tomorrowland station was mostly removed and the building closed off, but the Fantasyland station is still present. Many guests have seen the little chalet up on the hill behind and to the left of Casey Jr's Circus Train, but they don't know this was part of a great attraction. The building is now used occasionally for special events.

RIGHT: Although not the original shapes, the holes seen in the north and south sides of the Matterhorn are where the Skyway used to travel through it.

The Autopia has always been a popular attraction in all its various forms. After the renovation in 1959, the Autopia featured sporty, modern cars. These cars were eventually replaced during the 2000 renovation with the cars that are there now.

BELOW: From a trip to Disneyland in April 2007, I found one of the Mark VII cars, introduced in 1968, on display at the Disneyland Hotel. The car is in the lobby in front of Goofy's Kitchen and Steakhouse 55.

Mark VII Autopia vehicle, 1955-1999

The Mark VII model, which was introduced in 1968 by WED Enterprises (now Walt Disney Imagineering), represents the seventh style revolution and the third major body change in Autopia cars since they were introduced. The Mark VII is streamlined and low-slung, made of a unitized, fiberglass-reinforced, plastic body that features a stabilizing airfoil on the chopped-off rear end, giving it a "duck-tail" appearance. Drive power for the Mark VII is supplied by a mighty one-cylinder, air-cooled engine of seven horsepower. The Mark VII measures 109 inches long and 33 inches high, and weighs 830 pounds. The Autopia premiered on Disneyland's opening day, July 17, 1955 and is the only original Tomorrowland attraction still in existence today.

ABOVE AND BELOW: From June 1957 until January 1993, the Motor Boat Cruise navigated the waters of Fantasyland. Guests would board their boats from this dock. The boats can be thought of as Autopia on water. For the attraction's final eight months, it was converted to the Motor Boat Cruise to Gummi Glen in support of the Gummi Bear TV show (N: 57).

ABOVE: Full view of the Motor Boat Cruise dock from where Edelweiss Snack now stands.

ABOVE: Prior to being the Bibbidi Bobbidi Boutique, this store was the Tinker Bell Toy Shoppe, Once Upon a Time, and The Disney Princess Shoppe. Opening in 1957 between the walkway to Fantasy Faire princess meet and greet (Formerly Plaza Gardens) and Snow White's Scary Adventures dark attraction, this store carried a wide variety of toys, dolls, statues, and costumes. The store even had a storybook show where Disney princesses would come in and tell their story to children.

LEFT ABOVE, LEFT AND ABOVE: After being converted to the Bibbidi Bobbidi Boutique, three stowaways stayed behind. They can be seen under the eves on the main entrance. (N: 58)

The track for the People Mover (1967–1996)/Rocket Rods (1998–2000) attractions can still be seen all over Tomorrowland. Cast members have recently been seen on the tracks, meeting, and taking notes. Could they be thinking of bringing back the People Mover or making a new attraction? A presentation I attended in 2012 has convinced me it won't be the return of the People Mover, but it's still promising.

ABOVE: The loading area for the People Mover. You accessed this via an escalator located to the left. On top still sits the old

Rocket Jet base, now known as the Observatron.

RIGHT: View of the track and loading area from the Astro Orbitor.

ABOVE: Just past the Monorail beam you can see the People Mover tracks above Autopia. Look around Tomorrowland, the tracks can be seen in a lot of places.

RIGHT: View of the track from the loading area of the Monorail, where the track parallels the monorail tracks.

WOW !
That's Interesting

Most people who have read anything about the formation of Walt Disney's vision for Disneyland know that the seeds of the idea came to him while sitting on a bench in Griffith Park watching his daughters ride the merry-go-round. Below is the actual bench he sat on all those years ago, wishing there was a place he and his daughters could go to and enjoy attractions together. This bench sits in the entrance to Great Moments with Mr. Lincoln. There were many contributing ideas and experiences that lead to Disneyland, but I believe this is the critical one where it all started.

ABOVE: This is the plaque you see mounted on the bench in the center of the back rest.

From 2005 to 2010, there was a tradition for the two turkeys the President of the United States pardoned for Thanksgiving be given to Disneyland to live out the rest of their lives. After being pardoned, the turkies were flown first class aboard a commercial jet, designated "Turkey One," to Disneyland, where they would host the Thanksgiving parade. They had their own living area located at Big Thunder Ranch and were part of the Christmas season Reindeer Round-up. They could be seen at the entrance to Big Thunder Ranch on the walkway between Frontierland and Fantasyland. (N: 59)

ABOVE: First two Disneyland pardoned turkeys' from 2005: Marshmallow and Yamy.

ABOVE: The two pardoned turkeys from 2006: Flyer and Fryer.

ABOVE: Courage, who was pardoned in 2009.

Can you name all of the turkeys pardoned and given to Disneyland? (See note N: 60 for answers.)

LEFT: Sign from 2006 explaining the turkeys' pardons.

THE HAPPIEST TURKEYS ON EARTH!

EACH YEAR AT THANKSGIVING, THE PRESIDENT OF THE UNITED STATES "PARDONS" THE NATIONAL TURKEY DURING AN OFFICIAL WHITE HOUSE CEREMONY. THE PARDONED TURKEYS ARE THEN FLOWN ABOARD "TURKEY ONE" TO THE "HAPPIEST PLACE ON EARTH" TO BECOME THE HAPPIEST TURKEYS ON EARTH.

PLEASE WELCOME OUR NEW RANCH RESIDENTS!

RIGHT: Sign from 2005 explaining the turkeys' pardons.

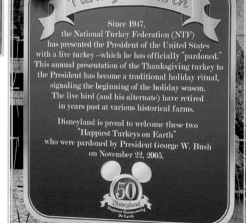

The Happiest Turkey on Earth

Since 1947, the National Turkey Federation (NTF) has presented the President of the United States with a live turkey —which he has officially "pardoned." This annual presentation of the Thanksgiving turkey to the President has become a traditional holiday ritual, signaling the beginning of the holiday season. The live bird (and his alternate) have retired in years past at various historical farms.

Disneyland is proud to welcome these two "Happiest Turkeys on Earth" who were pardoned by President George W. Bush on November 22, 2005.

Have you ever really looked at the gas street lamps that line Main Street U.S.A.? They were actually bought as scrap from Baltimore, Maryland, and St. Louis, Missouri for five cents a pound. All of the lamps weigh-in at around 500 pounds and each is over 150 years old. When Disneyland first opened, they were lit by hand each evening by a lamplighter in a traditional costume.

UPPER RIGHT CORNER: On December 22, 1982, Disneyland experienced a rare power outage. Guests were able to safely exit the Park due to the light emitted by the burning gas lamps. These lamps still work today, as seen in the picture. (N: 62/63)

LEFT AND RIGHT: There are many references to the flag pole in Town Square originally being a light post on Wilshire Boulevard in Los Angeles. Actually, it was only the base that was part of the famous light pole story. Disney Legend Emile Kuri saw that the light post had been knocked over in a traffic accident and he bought the damaged pole as scrap for five dollars. (N: 64)

Everyday at the flag retreat ceremony, the Disneyland Band and/or the Dapper Dans honor each branch of the armed services by asking former and present members to come forward and then plays/sings their service's official song. This tribute was still occurring as of April 2012.

LEFT: The plaque at the base of the flag pole features a transcript of Walt Disney's opening day speech.

142

LEFT AND BELOW: The giant palm tree to the right of the Jungle Cruise is one of the original trees located on the property when Walt Disney purchased the land in May of 1954. The tree is reported to have been planted in 1896 and, as such, is the oldest living thing on the Disneyland Resort. When Walt purchased the property he agreed to preserve the tree. The palm was moved from the original location to where it is planted today. During the renovation of the Jungle Cruise, a redesign of the new queue area had to be made in order to protect the tree. (N: 66 / 117)

Speaking of the Jungle Cruise, can you name all of the boats.? Here is a clue: there are 14 of them. (See note N: 107 for answer.)

ABOVE, LEFT AND BELOW: The tall grove of trees behind City Hall are all original trees to the property. They made a perfect barrier between the Jungle cruise and Main Street, so they were kept. The also added to the atmosphere of the Jungle Cruise. The stand of trees was planted as a wind break for the orange grove, which originally occupied the property. (N: 65)

Have you ever noticed the cats prowling around Disneyland? They are reportedly allowed to stay as they ironically help to keep down any rodent population. Don't worry kids, Mickey Mouse is in NO danger. Before the walk-through tour was added to Sleeping Beauty Castle, it was occupied by feral cats. Disneyland spays/neuters, feeds, provides shelters, and medical care for all the cats. (N: 67/98/99)

RIGHT: This cat was spotted walking on the old Mine Train through Nature's Wonderland tracks that run along Rivers of America. The cat was just in front of the old Mine Train through Nature's Wonderland engine. The engine has since been removed., but was located on the straight section of track.

ABOVE: This cat was on the old Mine Train through Nature's Wonderland tracks in front of the train abandoned on the tracks.

RIGHT: In foliage near Autopia, in Tomorrowland.

BELOW: This cat was on the hill above the train station, in Tomorrowland.

ABOVE: Have you noticed the side track or spur at the Main Street Disneyland Railroad station with the handcar? You may have thought the spur was just for looks or even to park trains occasionally. Parking trains is close to the real story. This spur was built during the original construction of Disneyland. They originally only had two trains, and they were allowed to pass each other here. Once they added a third train, passing was no longer allowed and a coordinated system was established to keep the trains moving, but at a safe distance from each other. (N: 69)

Can you name all five Disneyland Railroad engines? (N: 88)

LEFT: The cannons in Disneyland's Town Square are authentic cannons used by the French Army in the 19th century. They are reported to have never been fired in anger. (N: 61)

LEFT: Walk down East Center Street, the first alley on the right as you walk down Main Street U.S.A. towards Sleeping Beauty Castle. Just to the right of the rental locker area, you will see this "brick" wall. They are not really bricks, but are crafted to look like a brick wall. The Facade was constructed in 1954 to test the various types of faux bricks the Imagineers wanted to use around Disneyland. After completing their tests, a decision was made to leave the "test" wall in it current location as a novelty. (N: 71)

Recently, there has been some question as to whether this is the original wall or was replaced with a fiberglass duplicate. I spent some time with the wall in July 2013 and spoke to three cast members. All stated that it was the original wall. If you touch / tap the wall, you can clearly feel / hear that it is not fiberglass. The wood used to fill the center window is made out of fiberglass. I also compared it with known photographs of the original wall taken during the construction of Disneyland. The bottom white brick and corresponding red bricks were removed, but other than that, it appears to be the same wall. I believe it is the original wall, but even if it is not, it is still a duplicate of that famous wall.

ABOVE: You may have noticed all of the colorful shields hanging above you in the queue for the Matterhorn Bobsleds. You may have even thought, "Wow, they did a lot of work to create all the shields." Actually, the shields represent the coats of arms for each of the cantons (states) in Switzerland, the home of the real Matterhorn. For the 50th celebration, the white/blue/white shield (bottom row, second from left) was temporarily replaced with a 50th anniversary Mickey head. You can see his crest in the chapter on *Mickeys, Mickeys, Everywhere.* (N:70)

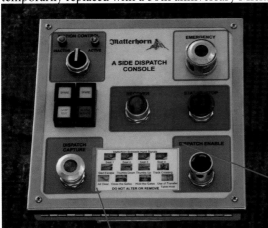

LEFT AND BELOW: You've probably heard the bells on the trains, gun shots on the Jungle Cruise, and the ships' horns. Did you know they all have very specific meanings? For instance, the horn on the Mark Twain signals the other watercraft its location. You've probably even seen the hand signals by operators. Did you know that there are more than just two or three hand signals most often seen? Some are universal and some are attraction specific. Here is a blow up of the hand signals used on the Matterhorn Bobsleds.

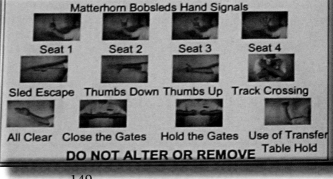

Matterhorn Bobsleds Hand Signals

Seat 1 Seat 2 Seat 3 Seat 4

Sled Escape Thumbs Down Thumbs Up Track Crossing

All Clear Close the Gates Hold the Gates Use of Transfer Table Hold

DO NOT ALTER OR REMOVE

LEFT AND BELOW: As you might expect, there are many rumors about Disneyland. One rumor is that many of the pirates in Pirates of the Caribbean are modeled after people who worked at The Walt Disney Studios, and that one is even a caricature of Walt Disney himself. I have spoken with an Imagineer who worked on the construction. I was told that only one pirate is modeled after a real person. One of the pirates in the scene with the dog is modeled after a janitor at The Walt Disney Studios. All of the other pirates are made up from various features of multiple people. Still, I have gone through the attraction many times looking to see if any of the pirates look anything like Walt Disney that would cause people to believe this rumor. If I had to choose a pirate to be Walt Disney, my money would be on this guy. He can be found standing next to the red head in the auction scene. (N: 108)

LEFT: This pumpkin head can be found in the pumpkin patch to the left of Goofy's house, in Mickey's Toontown. It is the only one that has glasses. It is in honor of Jack Lindquist, who worked for Disney from 1955 to 1993. From 1990 to 1993, he was the President of Disneyland. Heis sometimes referred to as the Mayor of Disneyland. Mr. Lindquist also has a window on Main Street and was named a Disney Legend in 1994. (N: 68)

BELOW AND NEXT TWO PAGES: I'm sure when riding the Big Thunder Mountain Railroad, most people have noticed the atmosphere has been enhanced by mining equipment. Disney has some of the best, if not the best, craftsmen, who can build anything. They can build ships, attractions, spaceships, cemeteries, themed buildings, animals, and even rocks. In this case, many of the artifacts "seen" lying around are real. Imagineering cast members went to old mines (in Wyoming, Nevada, Colorado, and Minnesota), ghost towns, and even swap meets to locate and purchase the old mining equipment. (N: 72)

BELOW TOP: The engine can be seen on the right side of the track at the start of hill 2.

BELOW BOTTOM: The ore cars on the left side just before starting up hill 3.

151

LEFT: This prop is located on the right side of the queue line just after the Fast Pass collection point.

RIGHT: This bucket is located on the left side of the tracks just after you start up the second hill. The gear you see is part of the hidden Mickey shown in the *Hidden Mickey* chapter of this book.

BELOW: These tools can be found to the right of the queue as you pass under the trestle just before gong up the stairs to the station.

ABOVE: This broken dinosaur egg can be seen in front of the dinosaur skeleton.

RIGHT: This gear is in the right queue line after you make the first switch back, just before going under the rock overhang.

LEFT: This gear and barrel can be seen leaning up against the Main Mine Shaft building in between the queue lines.

Bonus quiz: can you name the six train engines on Big Thunder Mountain Railroad? (See note N: 95 for answers.)

THIS PAGE AND NEXT: If you've been to the Enchanted Tiki Room, you've seen the masks and ornaments hanging in the walkway between the Central Plaza and Adventureland. You may have thought the Disney Imagineers and carpenters did a wonderful job creating the intricate masks. In reality, Walt Disney wanted these masks to be as authentic as possible. For this reason, he hired a firm called Oceanic Arts to make the realistic masks and other ornaments. This company has been providing Tiki items since 1956, and have supplied restaurants, amusement parks, the movie industry, and the general public. Other notable works include the thatched roofs on the Gilligan's Island TV series and the Vietnam village in the Forrest Gump movie. (N: 73)

Truly wonderful coloring and detail.

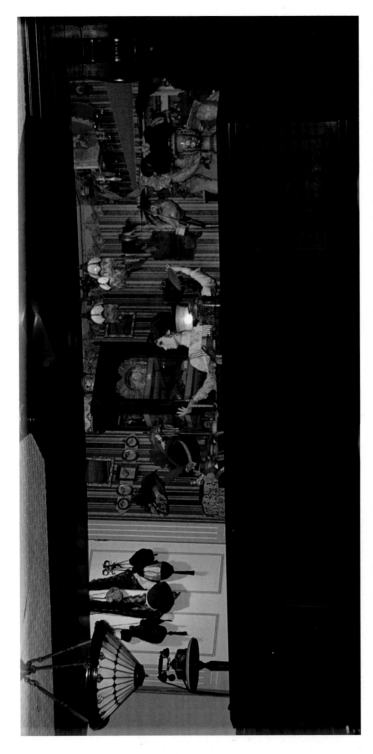

Most guests to Disneyland have visited the Emporium on Main Street. But have you ever looked up while shopping there? Located in the balconies are three scenes from the turn of the century. They are all themed to the time of Main Street U.S.A. .

ABOVE: A lady's hat and purse shop.

TOP AND MIDDLE: A tailor shop.

BOTTOM: A Barber Shop.

THIS PAGE: Of the 68 all-white prancing horses on the King Arthur Carrousel (plus seventeen spares), have you ever noticed the one with the gold tooth? This is rumored to have been Walt Disney's wife, Lillian's favorite horse. This has not been confirmed by Disneyland. (N: 74)

The carrousel itself is a handcrafted Dentzel that was made in 1922. It originally had many different types of animals in three rows. Additional horses were purchased and installed so everyone could ride a horse like King Arthur. A fourth row was also added to increase ridership. However, they were not all white originally. Eventually, due to the popularity of the white horses and "gallopers" on the attraction, all of the horses were converted to gallopers and painted white. (N: 75)

Each of the horses has a name. Can you name all 85 horses? You can get an official list at City Hall. (See note N: 97 for answers.)

RIGHT: Have you ever looked up at the windows in Fantasyland? The window above Snow White is a standard castle window with curtains drawn. Or is it? If you stand and watch for a couple of minutes, you might be surprised to see who looks out at the crowd periodically. The watcher is none other than the Evil Queen herself.

LEFT: At the end of the Tarzan Tree House tour, you will find a base camp. There you will see an old phonograph playing a scratchy song. Have you ever really listened to the song? It is the Swisskapolka, the song that used to played when the attraction was the Swiss Family Tree House.

ABOVE: Many people are aware that the room above the Disneyland Fire Station was Walt Disney's personal apartment. He would stay there when working late at Disneyland or entertaining guests.

Whenever he was in residence, a light was left on in the middle windows to let cast members know he was there. Since his passing on December 15, 1966, the light has always been left on all of the time, not only as a tribute, but also to let everyone know that Walt Disney is always present.

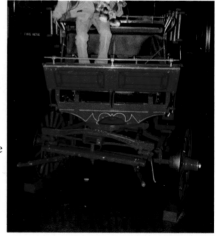

RIGHT: Many people have seen the fire engine inside the Disneyland Fire Station. Did you know that this old engine was actually a working attraction on opening day? It carried guests up and down Main Street. (N:109)

ABOVE AND LEFT: The fire pole in the rear of the fire station used to go up into Walt Disney's apartment. After one eager guest climbed up the pole and surprised the Disneys, the hole was sealed off to protect the apartment. Walt Disney is rumored to have occasionally used the pole to come down from his apartment until it was sealed. I could not confirm this. (N: 76)

Many of the attraction vehicles at Disneyland have common names such as trains, rockets, cars, ships, logs, horses, and bobsleds. But several have unique names. One of the first was the long-gone Adventure Thru Inner Space attraction. The attraction cars were called "Atomobiles" (not pictured). (N: 100)

ABOVE: On the Haunted Mansion, they are referred to as "Doom Buggies." (N: 102)

How many Doom Buggies are there? (See note N: 116 for answer.)

The generic term for the Adventure Thru Inner Space and Haunted Mansion attraction vehicle is Omnimover. Bob Gurr got the idea for the Omnimover looking at a candy apple on a stick. The general shape of the vehicle and the fact it rides on a central mounting post should look familiar to anyone who has eaten a candy apple. (N: 115)

ABOVE: Star Tours' Starspeeder 1000.

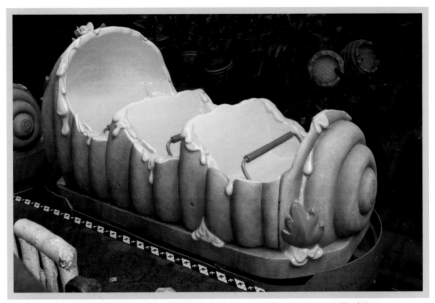

ABOVE: On the Many Adventures of Winnie the Pooh, they are called "Hunny Bee-Hives" or "Beehicles." (N: 111/101)

In addition, each of the Beehicles is named. Can you name them all? (See note N: 110 for answers.)

BELOW: On the Buzz Lightyear Astro Blasters, they are known as "XP-40 Space Cruisers." (N: 103)

ABOUT THE AUTHOR

ABOVE: The author enjoying one of his favorite Disneyland treats, beignets. This one is from the French Market Restaurant at the Mint Julep Bar and is shaped like Mickey.

Russell was born and raised on the Central California Coast. Living only three-and-a-half hours from Disneyland, Russell was fortunate enough to get to visit Disneyland several times a year while growing up. From 1968 to 1980, he visited Disneyland over 36 times. After that, he only visited Disneyland once a year or so until the birth of his only child. In 1991, Russell met his future wife and in 1993 they were married. She is also a big fan of Disneyland. They went to Disneyland twice before getting married. For their honeymoon, they went to Walt Disney World. It was the first trip for both of them. In 1995 they moved to Sacramento. They were then seven hours from Disneyland, making trips only once every few years. In 2000 they had their one and only child. Russell and his wife, wanting their child to share in the same joys of going to Disneyland as they had as children, starting taking her at age three. That year they took two trips and quickly bought annual passes and a stone marker in the Esplanade. They also discovered that to make the travel easier, they would go for one week trips rather than more frequent shorter trips. This lead to their twice-a-year trip schedule. In 2008 they all went to Walt Disney World for Russ and his wife's fifteenth wedding anniversary. They are also fortunate enough to have several friends who are also Disney fans. They enjoy taking trips with friends and family, as well as trips by themselves. They have visited the Disney Family Museum in San Francisco and the Disney Studios in Burbank. They also enjoy participating in Disneyland events such as the Disneyland Half Marathon, Mickey's Very Merry Christmas Party (Walt Disney World), Mickey's Not So Scary Halloween Party (Disneyland), Be Our Guest Dinner, and Pacific Northwest Mouse Meet. They are Disneyland Annual Pass Holders, Disney Vacation Club (DVC) members and D23 members.

Follow us on our web page, FaceBook and Twitter for more information about future books in the series. Watch for *More Seen, Un-Seen Disneyland*, and *Seen, Un-Seen Disneyland: California Adventure Edition*.

Facebook

http://www.facebook.com/seenunseendisneyland

The Web
http://www.sudbooks.com

Twitter

http://www.twitter.com/seenunseend

NOTES

#1 Kevin Yee and Jason Schultz, 101 Things You Never Knew About Disneyland: An Unauthorized Look at the Little Touches and Inside Jokes (Orlando: Zauberreich Press, 2005-2007), #77

#2 Kevin Yee and Jason Schultz, 101 Things You Never Knew About Disneyland: An Unauthorized Look at the Little Touches and Inside Jokes (Orlando: Zauberreich Press, 2005-2007), #77

#3 Kevin Yee and Jason Schultz, 101 Things You Never Knew About Disneyland: An Unauthorized Look at the Little Touches and Inside Jokes (Orlando: Zauberreich Press, 2005-2007), #77

#4 Kevin Yee and Jason Schultz, 101 Things You Never Knew About Disneyland: An Unauthorized Look at the Little Touches and Inside Jokes (Orlando: Zauberreich Press, 2005-2007), #77

#5 Kevin Yee and Jason Schultz, 101 Things You Never Knew About Disneyland: An Unauthorized Look at the Little Touches and Inside Jokes (Orlando: Zauberreich Press, 2005-2007), #77

#6 Kevin Yee and Jason Schultz, 101 Things You Never Knew About Disneyland: An Unauthorized Look at the Little Touches and Inside Jokes (Orlando: Zauberreich Press, 2005-2007), #77

#7 Bruce Gordon and Tim O'Day, Disneyland: Then, Now and Forever (New York: Disney Editions, 2005 and 2008 Editions), p. 111.

Kendra Trahan, Disneyland Detective: An INDEPENDENT Guide to Discovering Disney's Legend, Lore, and Magic! 50th
Anniversary Update (Mission Viejo: PermaGrin Publishing, Inc., 2005), p. 144.

Chris Strodder, The Disneyland Encyclopedia: The UNOfficial, UNAuthorized, and UNPrecedented History of Every Land,
Attraction, Restaurant, Shop, and Event in the Original Magic Kingdom (Santa Monica. Santa Monica Press LLC., 2008),
p. 271 – 272.

#8 David Hoffman, Little-Known FACTS about Well-Known PLACES Disneyland (New York: Metro Books, 2008), p. 44.

Kevin Yee and Jason Schultz, 101 Things You Never Knew About Disneyland: An Unauthorized Look at the Little Touches and Inside Jokes (Orlando: Zauberreich Press, 2005-2007), #73.

Bruce Gordon and Tim O'Day, Disneyland: Then, Now and Forever (New York: Disney Editions, 2005 and 2008 Editions),
p. 39.

Kendra Trahan, Disneyland Detective: An INDEPENDENT Guide to Discovering Disney's Legend, Lore, and Magic! 50th Anniversary Update (Mission Viejo: PermaGrin Publishing, Inc., 2005), p. 127.

#9 Kevin Yee and Jason Schultz, 101 Things You Never Knew About Disneyland: An Unauthorized Look at the Little
Touches and Inside Jokes (Orlando: Zauberreich Press, 2005-2007), Postscript: Untrue Urban Legends.

#10 Jim Flanning, Disneyland Challenge (New York: Disney Editions, 2009), Sleeping Beauty Castle Section.

Bruce Gordon and Tim O'Day, Disneyland: Then, Now and Forever (New York: Disney Editions, 2005 and 2008 Editions),
p. 39.

#11 HiddenMickeys.org, Fun Facts of Disneyland's Sleeping Beauty Castle, http://www. hiddenmickeys.org/Disneyland/Secrets/Fantasy/Castle.html (9/28/2010).

William Silvester, Disney's Sleeping Beauty Castle, http://www.suite101.com/content/ sleeping-beauty-castle-a47210 (9/29/2010).

#12 Chris Strodder, The Disneyland Encyclopedia: The UNOfficial, UNAuthorized, and UNPrecedented History of Every Land, Attraction, Restaurant, Shop, and Event in the Original Magic Kingdom (Santa Monica. Santa Monica Press LLC., 2008), p. 377-379.

Kendra Trahan, Disneyland Detective: An INDEPENDENT Guide to Discovering Disney's Legend, Lore, and Magic! 50th Anniversary Update (Mission Viejo: PermaGrin Publishing, Inc., 2005), p. 126.

#13 Chris Strodder, The Disneyland Encyclopedia: The UNOfficial, UNAuthorized, and UNPrecedented History of Every Land, Attraction, Restaurant, Shop, and Event in the Original Magic Kingdom (Santa Monica. Santa Monica Press LLC., 2008), p. 379-380.

Kendra Trahan, Disneyland Detective: An INDEPENDENT Guide to Discovering Disney's Legend, Lore, and Magic! 50th Anniversary Update (Mission Viejo: PermaGrin Publishing, Inc., 2005), p. 126.

Daveland.com, Sleeping Beauty Diorama, from http://davelandweb.com/castle/ diorama.html (7/19/2010)

#14 David Hoffman, Little-Known FACTS about Well-Known PLACES Disneyland (New York: Metro Books, 2008), p. 160.

#15 David Hoffman, Little-Known FACTS about Well-Known PLACES Disneyland (New York: Metro Books, 2008), p. 94.

Smith, Dave, Chief Archivist Emeritus, Walt Disney Archives.

#16 Daveland.com, Tell-No-Tales Thursdays: Entrance Queue Murals, http://davelandblog.blogspot.com/2009/06/tell-no-tales-thursdays-entrance-queue.html (June 18, 2009)

#17 Chris Strodder, The Disneyland Encyclopedia: The UNOfficial, UNAuthorized, and UNPrecedented History of Every Land, Attraction, Restaurant, Shop, and Event in the Original Magic Kingdom (Santa Monica. Santa Monica Press LLC., 2008), p. 332-334.

Jason Surrell, Pirates of the Caribbean: From the Magic Kingdom to the Movies (New York. Disney Editions, 2005), p. 98.

#18 Minnie Mouse is short for Minerva Mouse.

Walt Disney's Comics and Stories: No. 688 January 2008 (USA: Gemstone Publishing, 2008}, p. 13.

Mickeypedia.com, Minnie Mouse, http://www.mickeypedia.com/articles/Disney/Minnie_Mouse.html (9/27/2010).

Facebook.com, Minnie Mouse, http://www.facebook.com/#!/pages/Minnie-Mouse/112067295472969?ref=ts (9/28/2010).

Facebook.com, Minnie Mouse, http://www.facebook.com/isneyMinnieMouse?sk=info (12/9/2011).

#19 Amy Booth Green and Howard G. Green, Remembering Walt: Favorite Memories of Walt Disney (New York: Disney Enterprises, Inc., 1999), p. 156, John Hench.

#20 Jim Flanning, Disneyland Challenge (New York: Disney Editions, 2009), Roger Rabbit Car Toon Spin section.

Roger Rabbit License plates:

2N TOWN (Toontown)	BB WOLF (Big Bad Wolf)
MR TOAD (Mr. Toad)	1DRLND (Wonderland)
1D N PTR (Wendy & Peter Pan)	IM L8 (I'm late - The White Rabbit)
CAP 10 HK (Captain Hook)	L MERM8 (The Little Mermaid)
101 DLMN (101 Dalmatians)	FAN T C (Fantasy)
RS2CAT (Aristocat)	ZPD2DA (Zip-a-dee-doo-dah)
3 LIL PIGS (Three Little Pigs)	

#21 Kevin Yee and Jason Schultz, 101 Things You Never Knew About Disneyland: An Unauthorized Look at the Little Touches and Inside Jokes (Orlando: Zauberreich Press, 2005-2007), #94.

Kendra Trahan, Disneyland Detective: An INDEPENDENT Guide to Discovering Disney's Legend, Lore, and Magic! 50th

Anniversary Update (Mission Viejo: PermaGrin Publishing, Inc., 2005), p. 172 (Treasure & Trivia).

David Hoffman, Little-Known FACTS about Well-Known PLACES Disneyland (New York: Metro Books, 2008), p. 130.

#22 Kevin Yee and Jason Schultz, 101 Things You Never Knew About Disneyland: An Unauthorized Look at the Little Touches and Inside Jokes (Orlando: Zauberreich Press, 2005-2007), #23.

#23 Kendra Trahan, Disneyland Detective: An INDEPENDENT Guide to Discovering Disney's Legend, Lore, and Magic! 50th Anniversary Update (Mission Viejo: PermaGrin Publishing, Inc., 2005), p. 113.

Kevin Yee and Jason Schultz, 101 Things You Never Knew About Disneyland: An Unauthorized Look at the Little Touches and Inside Jokes (Orlando: Zauberreich Press, 2005-2007), #63.

...and the winner is? Looking at the original movie, the numbers did not go all the way up the smoke stacks. For that reason, it appears that the engine in the back has had its number changed. In addition, it would be most proper to have the winning engine up front. For these reason, the author believes that the engine in front was the winner.

#24 Kevin Yee and Jason Schultz, 101 Things You Never Knew About Disneyland: An Unauthorized Look at the Little Touches and Inside Jokes (Orlando: Zauberreich Press, 2005-2007), #48.

#25 Kendra Trahan, Disneyland Detective: An INDEPENDENT Guide to Discovering Disney's Legend, Lore, and Magic! 50th Anniversary Update (Mission Viejo: PermaGrin Publishing, Inc., 2005), p. 124-125.

Jason Surrell, The Haunted Mansion: From Magic Kingdom to the Movies (New York. Disney Editions, 2003),
p. 77.

Kevin Yee and Jason Schultz, 101 Things You Never Knew About Disneyland: An Unauthorized Look at the Little Touches and Inside Jokes (Orlando: Zauberreich Press, 2005-2007), #40

Bruce Gordon and Tim O'Day, Disneyland: Then, Now and Forever (New York: Disney Editions, 2005 and 2008 Editions),
p. 124/125.

#26 Kevin Yee and Jason Schultz, 101 Things You Never Knew About Disneyland: An Unauthorized Look at the Little Touches and Inside Jokes (Orlando: Zauberreich Press, 2005-2007), #45.

Bruce Gordon and Tim O'Day, Disneyland: Then, Now and Forever (New York: Disney Editions, 2005 and 2008 Editions), p. 142.

#27 Kevin Yee and Jason Schultz, 101 Things You Never Knew About Disneyland: An Unauthorized Look at the Little Touches and Inside Jokes (Orlando: Zauberreich Press, 2005-2007), #93

Bruce Gordon and Tim O'Day, Disneyland: Then, Now and Forever (New York: Disney Editions, 2005 and 2008 Editions),
p. 142.

#28 Kevin Yee and Jason Schultz, 101 Things You Never Knew About Disneyland: An Unauthorized Look at the Little Touches and Inside Jokes (Orlando: Zauberreich Press, 2005-2007), #94.

#29 Kevin Yee and Jason Schultz, 101 Things You Never Knew About Disneyland: An Unauthorized Look at the Little Touches and Inside Jokes (Orlando: Zauberreich Press, 2005-2007), #94.

#30 Kevin Yee and Jason Schultz, 101 Things You Never Knew About Disneyland: An Unauthorized Look at the Little Touches and Inside Jokes (Orlando: Zauberreich Press, 2005-2007), #66.

Kendra Trahan, Disneyland Detective: An INDEPENDENT Guide to Discovering Disney's Legend, Lore, and Magic! 50th Anniversary Update (Mission Viejo: PermaGrin Publishing, Inc., 2005), p. 106.

#31 Kevin Yee and Jason Schultz, 101 Things You Never Knew About Disneyland: An Unauthorized Look at the Little Touches and Inside Jokes (Orlando: Zauberreich Press, 2005-2007), #66.

#32 Kevin Yee and Jason Schultz, 101 Things You Never Knew About Disneyland: An Unauthorized Look at the Little Touches and Inside Jokes (Orlando: Zauberreich Press, 2005-2007), #66.

Kendra Trahan, Disneyland Detective: An INDEPENDENT Guide to Discovering Disney's Legend, Lore, and Magic! 50th Anniversary Update (Mission Viejo: PermaGrin Publishing, Inc., 2005), p. 106.

#33 Kevin Yee and Jason Schultz, 101 Things You Never Knew About Disneyland: An Unauthorized Look at the Little Touches and Inside Jokes (Orlando: Zauberreich Press, 2005-2007), #66.

#34 Kevin Yee and Jason Schultz, 101 Things You Never Knew About Disneyland: An Unauthorized Look at the Little Touches and Inside Jokes (Orlando: Zauberreich Press, 2005-2007), #65.

#35 Kevin Yee and Jason Schultz, 101 Things You Never Knew About Disneyland: An Unauthorized Look at the Little Touches and Inside Jokes (Orlando: Zauberreich Press, 2005-2007), #62.

Jim Flanning, Disneyland Challenge (New York: Disney Editions, 2009), Big Thunder Mountain Railroad section.

#36 Kevin Yee and Jason Schultz, 101 Things You Never Knew About Disneyland: An Unauthorized Look at the Little Touches and Inside Jokes (Orlando: Zauberreich Press, 2005-2007), #66.

Kendra Trahan, Disneyland Detective: An INDEPENDENT Guide to Discovering Disney's Legend, Lore, and Magic! 50th Anniversary Update (Mission Viejo: PermaGrin Publishing, Inc., 2005), p. 70-71.

#37 Daveland.com, Daveland Disneyland Astrojets Photo Page, http://davelandweb. com/astrojets/ (9/29/2010).

MiceChat.com. What was the Observatron, http://micechat.com/forums/disneyland-resort/3475-what-observatron.html (9/29/2010).

Yesterdayland.com, Rocket Jets at Yesterland, http://www.yesterland.com/rocketjets. html (9/29/2010).

#38 Kevin Yee and Jason Schultz, 101 Things You Never Knew About Disneyland: An Unauthorized Look at the Little Touches and Inside Jokes (Orlando: Zauberreich Press, 2005-2007), #55.

Chris Strodder, The Disneyland Encyclopedia: The UNOfficial, UNAuthorized, and UNPrecedented History of Every Land, Attraction, Restaurant, Shop, and Event in the Original Magic Kingdom (Santa Monica. Santa Monica Press LLC., 2008), p. 284 – 285.

During the 2010 refurbishment of the Rivers of America, the Gullywhumper was moved from the location in the picture to its present location in front of Mike Fink's cabin.

#39 Chris Strodder, The Disneyland Encyclopedia: The UNOfficial, UNAuthorized, and UNPrecedented History of Every Land, Attraction, Restaurant, Shop, and Event in the Original Magic Kingdom (Santa Monica. Santa Monica Press LLC., 2008), p. 292 – 294.

#40 Kevin Yee and Jason Schultz, 101 Things You Never Knew About Disneyland: An Unauthorized Look at the Little Touches and Inside Jokes (Orlando: Zauberreich Press, 2005-2007), #101.

#41 Green, Amy Booth and Howard G. Green, Remembering Walt: Favorite Memories of Walt Disney (New York: Disney Enterprises, Inc., 1999), p. 2.

Whitney Stewart. Who Was Walt Disney? (New York: Penguin Group (USA), Inc., 2009), p 4 - 10.

#42 Chris Strodder, The Disneyland Encyclopedia: The UNOfficial, UNAuthorized, and UNPrecedented History of Every Land, Attraction, Restaurant, Shop, and Event in the Original Magic Kingdom (Santa Monica. Santa Monica Press LLC., 2008), p. 214.

Kevin Yee and Jason Schultz, 101 Things You Never Knew About Disneyland: An Unauthorized Look at the Little Touches and Inside Jokes (Orlando: Zauberreich Press, 2005-2007), #43.

#43 Chris Strodder, The Disneyland Encyclopedia: The UNOfficial, UNAuthorized, and UNPrecedented History of Every Land, Attraction, Restaurant, Shop, and Event in the Original Magic Kingdom (Santa Monica. Santa Monica Press LLC., 2008), p. 265.

#44 Kevin Yee and Jason Schultz, 101 Things You Never Knew About Disneyland: An Unauthorized Look at the Little Touches and Inside Jokes (Orlando: Zauberreich Press, 2005-2007), #70.

#45 Kevin Yee and Jason Schultz, 101 Things You Never Knew About Disneyland: An Unauthorized Look at the Little Touches and Inside Jokes (Orlando: Zauberreich Press, 2005-2007), #35.

#46 Kevin Yee and Jason Schultz, 101 Things You Never Knew About Disneyland: An Unauthorized Look at the Little Touches and Inside Jokes (Orlando: Zauberreich Press, 2005-2007), #95.

#47 Kevin Yee and Jason Schultz, 101 Things You Never Knew About Disneyland: An Unauthorized Look at the Little Touches and Inside Jokes (Orlando: Zauberreich Press, 2005-2007), #95.

#48 Kevin Yee and Jason Schultz, 101 Things You Never Knew About Disneyland: An Unauthorized Look at the Little Touches and Inside Jokes (Orlando: Zauberreich Press, 2005-2007), #48

#49 Kevin Yee and Jason Schultz, 101 Things You Never Knew About Disneyland: An Unauthorized Look at the Little Touches and Inside Jokes (Orlando: Zauberreich Press, 2005-2007), #24.

Jim Flanning, Disneyland Challenge (New York: Disney Editions, 2009), Tarzan's Treehouse section.

#50 Jim Flanning, Disneyland Challenge (New York: Disney Editions, 2009), "By the numbers" Challenge section.

#51 The Imagineers, Walt Disney Imagineering: A Behind the Dreams Look at Making MORE Magic Real,(New York , Disney Editions, 2010) p. 87.

#52 MouseBuzz.com, Secret bathroom at DL?, http://www.mousebuzz.com/forum/disneyland-theme-parks/49179-secret-bathroom-dl.html (9/25/2010).

Visionsfantastic.com. Secret Bathroom, http://www.visionsfantastic.com/forum/f52/secret-bathroom-9492/ (9/25/2010)

MousePlanet.com, The Secret Bathroom, http://mousepad.mouseplanet.com/showthread.php?t=53169&goto=nextoldest (9/25/2010)

MousePlanet.com. I need a picture of the entry/walkway to the secret bathroom! . http://mousepad.mouseplanet.com/showthread.php?t=144399&highlight=secret+bathroom (9/29/2010).

The secret bathroom was located in the back corner of the Princess "Meet & Greet" area (formerly the Garden Plaza Stage area). If you were in the Princess "Meet & Greet" area and started to walk to Rancho del Zocalos Restaurante through the wooden walkway, you would see it off to the right just before you entered the covered walkway. It was removed with the plussing of the area to the new Princess "Meet & Greet" area. The bathroom in the Tahitian Terrace is the new family bathroom.

#53 The first time was for opening day, July 17, 1955. The second time was on the re-dedication day of Fantasyland in 1983.

Kendra Trahan, Disneyland Detective: An INDEPENDENT Guide to Discovering Disney's Legend, Lore, and Magic! 50th Anniversary Update (Mission Viejo: PermaGrin Publishing, Inc., 2005), p. 126.

#54 Kevin Yee and Jason Schultz, 101 Things You Never Knew About Disneyland: An Unauthorized Look at the Little Touches and Inside Jokes (Orlando: Zauberreich Press, 2005-2007), #33

Disneylandclub33.com, How Do I Join?, http://www.disneylandclub33.com/How-Do_I-Join.htm (9/25/2010).

Disneylandclub33.com, Welcome To Our Club 33 Home Page, http://www.disneylandclub33.com/index.html (9/25/2010).

#55 David Koenig, More Mouse Tales: A Closer Peek Backstage At Disneyland,(Irvine, Bonaventure Press, 2002) p. 50.

#56 Chris Strodder, The Disneyland Encyclopedia: The UNOfficial, UNAuthorized, and UNPrecedented History of Every Land, Attraction, Restaurant, Shop, and Event in the Original Magic Kingdom (Santa Monica. Santa Monica Press LLC., 2008), p. 375.

#57 Chris Strodder, The Disneyland Encyclopedia: The UNOfficial, UNAuthorized, and UNPrecedented History of Every Land, Attraction, Restaurant, Shop, and Event in the Original Magic Kingdom (Santa Monica. Santa Monica Press LLC., 2008), p. 294 – 295.

#58 Chris Strodder, The Disneyland Encyclopedia: The UNOfficial, UNAuthorized, and UNPrecedented History of Every Land, Attraction, Restaurant, Shop, and Event in the Original Magic Kingdom (Santa Monica. Santa Monica Press LLC., 2008), p. 414 -415

#59 David Hoffman, Little-Known FACTS about Well-Known PLACES Disneyland (New York: Metro Books, 2008), p. 34.

Borgna Brunner and Mark Hughes, Presidential Pardon: The turkey that lives to see another day, http://www.infoplease.com/spot/tgturkey2.html (April 23, 2010)

#60 Borgna Brunner and Mark Hughes, Presidential Pardon: The turkey that lives to see another day, http://www.infoplease.com/spot/tgturkey2.html (April 23, 2010)

Alexander C. Hart, Los Angeles Times, Pardoned turkeys off to Disneyland, http://articles.latimes.com/2009/nov/26/nation/la-na-turkey-pardon26-2009nov26 (September 28, 2010)

2005	Marshmallow and Yamy
2006	Flyer and Fryer
2007	May and Flower
2008	Pumpkin and Pecan
2009	Courage and Carolina

#61 Kevin Yee and Jason Schultz, 101 Things You Never Knew About Disneyland: An Unauthorized Look at the Little Touches and Inside Jokes (Orlando: Zauberreich Press, 2005-2007), #

Jim Flanning, Disneyland Challenge (New York: Disney Editions, 2009), Main Street U.S.A. section.

David Hoffman, Little-Known FACTS about Well-Known PLACES Disneyland (New York: Metro Books, 2008), p. 78.

#62 Kevin Yee and Jason Schultz, 101 Things You Never Knew About Disneyland: An Unauthorized Look at the Little Touches and Inside Jokes (Orlando: Zauberreich Press, 2005-2007), #5.

Jim Flanning, Disneyland Challenge (New York: Disney Editions, 2009), Main Street U.S.A. section.

David Hoffman, Little-Known FACTS about Well-Known PLACES Disneyland (New York: Metro Books, 2008), p. 79.

Kendra Trahan, Disneyland Detective: An INDEPENDENT Guide to Discovering Disney's Legend, Lore, and Magic! 50th Anniversary Update (Mission Viejo: PermaGrin Publishing, Inc., 2005), p. 12.

#63 Kevin Yee and Jason Schultz, 101 Things You Never Knew About Disneyland: An Unauthorized Look at the Little Touches and Inside Jokes (Orlando: Zauberreich Press, 2005-2007), #5.

David Hoffman, Little-Known FACTS about Well-Known PLACES Disneyland (New York: Metro Books, 2008), p. 79.

#64 David Hoffman, Little-Known FACTS about Well-Known PLACES Disneyland (New York: Metro Books, 2008), p. 77.

Kendra Trahan, Disneyland Detective: An INDEPENDENT Guide to Discovering Disney's Legend, Lore, and Magic! 50th Anniversary Update (Mission Viejo: PermaGrin Publishing, Inc., 2005), p. 12.

#65 Kevin Yee and Jason Schultz, 101 Things You Never Knew About Disneyland: An Unauthorized Look at the Little Touches and Inside Jokes (Orlando: Zauberreich Press, 2005-2007), #8.

David Hoffman, Little-Known FACTS about Well-Known PLACES Disneyland (New York: Metro Books, 2008), p. 145.

Kendra Trahan, Disneyland Detective: An INDEPENDENT Guide to Discovering Disney's Legend, Lore, and Magic! 50th Anniversary Update (Mission Viejo: PermaGrin Publishing, Inc., 2005), p. 13.

#66 Kevin Yee and Jason Schultz, 101 Things You Never Knew About Disneyland: An Unauthorized Look at the Little Touches and Inside Jokes (Orlando: Zauberreich Press, 2005-2007), #18

#67 David Hoffman, Little-Known FACTS about Well-Known PLACES Disneyland (New York: Metro Books, 2008), p. 48.

#68 Jim Flanning, Disneyland Challenge (New York: Disney Editions, 2009), Goofy's Playhouse section.

#69 Kevin Yee and Jason Schultz, 101 Things You Never Knew About Disneyland: An Unauthorized Look at the Little Touches and Inside Jokes (Orlando: Zauberreich Press, 2005-2007), #3.

Disney.wikia.com, Disneyland Railroad, http://disney.wiki.com/wiki/Disneyland_Railroad (10/3/2010).

Wikipedia.com, Disneyland Railroad, http://en.wikipedia.org/wiki/Disneyland_Railroad (5/9/2010).

#70 Kendra Trahan, Disneyland Detective: An INDEPENDENT Guide to Discovering Disney's Legend, Lore, and Magic! 50th Anniversary Update (Mission Viejo: PermaGrin Publishing, Inc., 2005), p. 144.

#71 Jeff Baham, 5 Disneyland secrets that nobody knows, http://www.examiner.com/x-10719-Disney-Theme-Parks-Examiner~y2009m6d30-5-Disneyland-secrets-that-nobody-knows (April 23, 2010).

#72 Kevin Yee and Jason Schultz, 101 Things You Never Knew About Disneyland: An Unauthorized Look at the Little Touches and Inside Jokes (Orlando: Zauberreich Press, 2005-2007), #63.

Jim Flanning, Disneyland Challenge (New York: Disney Editions, 2009), Big Thunder Mountain Railroad section.

Allears.net, Big Thunder Mountain Railroad - Frontierland, Disneyland, http://allears.net/dlr/tp/dl/btmrr.htm (1/22/2012).

#73 Tiki Central, Oceanic Arts, Whittier, CA , http://www.tikiroom.com/tikicentral/bb/viewtopic.php?topic=7252&forum=2 (5/4/2010).

Daveland.com, Daveland@Disneyland A-Z: Adventureland Gate, http://www.2719hyperion.com/2009/02/davelanddisneyland-in-photos-az.html (May 4, 2010).

Oceanic Arts, Humuhumu's Description, http://www.critiki.com/cgi-bin/location.cgi?loc_id=202 (May 3, 2010).

#74 Kevin Yee and Jason Schultz, 101 Things You Never Knew About Disneyland: An Unauthorized Look at the Little Touches and Inside Jokes (Orlando: Zauberreich Press, 2005-2007), Postscript: Untrue Urban Legends.

Kendra Trahan, Disneyland Detective: An INDEPENDENT Guide to Discovering Disney's Legend, Lore, and Magic! 50th Anniversary Update (Mission Viejo: PermaGrin Publishing, Inc., 2005), p. 129.

#75 Kevin Yee and Jason Schultz, 101 Things You Never Knew About Disneyland: An Unauthorized Look at the Little Touches and Inside Jokes (Orlando: Zauberreich Press, 2005-2007), #71.

Chris Strodder, The Disneyland Encyclopedia: The UNOfficial, UNAuthorized, and UNPrecedented History of Every Land, Attraction, Restaurant, Shop, and Event in the Original Magic Kingdom (Santa Monica. Santa Monica Press LLC., 2008), p. 233 – 234.

#76 Kendra Trahan, Disneyland Detective: An INDEPENDENT Guide to Discovering Disney's Legend, Lore, and Magic! 50th Anniversary Update (Mission Viejo: PermaGrin Publishing, Inc., 2005), p. 14.

David Wallace, Disneyland Trivia: Walt Disney's Apartment, http://www.davidwallace.com/2007/09/disneyland-trivia-walt-disneys-apartment/ (9/29/2010).

FindingMickey.com, Disneyland Facts & History > Main Street U. S. A., http://findingmickey.squarespace.com/disneyland-facts/main-street-usa/ (9/29/2010).

#77 Kevin Yee and Jason Schultz, 101 Things You Never Knew About Disneyland: An Unauthorized Look at the Little Touches and Inside Jokes (Orlando: Zauberreich Press, 2005-2007), #44

Kendra Trahan, Disneyland Detective: An INDEPENDENT Guide to Discovering Disney's Legend, Lore, and Magic! 50th Anniversary Update (Mission Viejo: PermaGrin Publishing, Inc., 2005), p. 46.

Chris Strodder, The Disneyland Encyclopedia: The UNOfficial, UNAuthorized, and UNPrecedented History of Every Land, Attraction, Restaurant, Shop, and Event in the Original Magic Kingdom (Santa Monica. Santa Monica Press LLC., 2008), p. 265.

Bruce Gordon and Tim O'Day, Disneyland: Then, Now and Forever (New York: Disney Editions, 2005 and 2008 Editions), p. 46.

#78 Jim Flanning, Disneyland Challenge (New York: Disney Editions, 2009), Big Thunder Mountain Railroad section.

#79 September 18, 2010: A guide at the Disney Family Museum told me that the train and cars are at the Disney Archives for preservation. It is unknown if they will be returned.

#80 Kevin Yee and Jason Schultz, 101 Things You Never Knew About Disneyland: An Unauthorized Look at the Little Touches and Inside Jokes (Orlando: Zauberreich Press, 2005-2007), #101.

#81 David Hoffman, Little-Known FACTS about Well-Known PLACES Disneyland (New York: Metro Books, 2008), p. 103.

#82 Kevin Yee and Jason Schultz, 101 Things You Never Knew About Disneyland: An Unauthorized Look at the Little Touches and Inside Jokes (Orlando: Zauberreich Press, 2005-2007), #49

George Eldridge, Decoding the Disneyland Telegraph, http://www.hiddenmickeys.org/ Disneyland/Secrets/Square/Morse.html (April 23, 2010).

#83 Jeff Baham, 5 Disneyland secrets that nobody knows , http://www.examiner.com/x-10719-Disney-Theme-Parks-Examiner~y2009m6d30-5-Disneyland-secrets-that-nobody-knows (April 23, 2010).

#84 Rockets Astro Jets 3/1956 to 1964
       Tomorrowland Jets 8/1964 to 9/1966
       Rocket Jets 7/67 to 1/97
       New base a rockets now called Astro Orbitor 1998 to present
       Original base is now Observatron

#85 David Hoffman, Little-Known FACTS about Well-Known PLACES Disneyland (New York: Metro Books, 2008), p. 107.

#86 Kevin Yee and Jason Schultz, 101 Things You Never Knew About Disneyland: An Unauthorized Look at the Little Touches and Inside Jokes (Orlando: Zauberreich Press, 2005-2007), Postscript: Untrue Urban Legends.

#87 Kevin Yee and Jason Schultz, 101 Things You Never Knew About Disneyland: An Unauthorized Look at the Little Touches and Inside Jokes (Orlando: Zauberreich Press, 2005-2007), #74

#88 Kevin Yee and Jason Schultz, 101 Things You Never Knew About Disneyland: An Unauthorized Look at the Little Touches and Inside Jokes (Orlando: Zauberreich Press, 2005-2007), #2.

The first four engines were named after Santa Fe railroad executives. They are:

> #1 C.K. Holliday (founder) (began operations opening day, July 17, 1955)
> #2 E.P. Ripley (first president) (began operations opening day, July 17, 1955)
> #3 Fred Gurley (Chairman 1955) (began operations March 28, 1958)
> #4 Ernest S. Marsh (President 1955) (began operations July 25, 1959)

The fifth engine was added in June 25, 2005. It is named the Ward Kimball. It is named after Mr. Ward Kimball a famous Imagineer who loved trains like Walt Disney.

#89 DisneylandNews.com, Disneyland Fun Facts, http://www.disneylandnews.com/fact+sheets+and+more/background/disneyland+park+fun+facts.htm (September 28, 2010).

#90 Kendra Trahan, Disneyland Detective: An INDEPENDENT Guide to Discovering Disney's Legend, Lore, and Magic! 50th Anniversary Update (Mission Viejo: PermaGrin Publishing, Inc., 2005), p. 125.

#91 Allears.net, Cinderella Castle - Magic Kingdom, http://allears.net/tp/mk/castle.htm (9/28/2010).

#92 Gordon, Bruce and Tim O'Day, Disneyland: Then, Now and Forever (New York: Disney Editions, 2005 and 2008 Editions), p. 39.

#93 Gordon, Bruce and Tim O'Day, Disneyland: Then, Now and Forever (New York: Disney Editions, 2005 and 2008 Editions), p. 39.

Kendra Trahan, Disneyland Detective: An INDEPENDENT Guide to Discovering Disney's Legend, Lore, and Magic! 50th Anniversary Update (Mission Viejo: PermaGrin Publishing, Inc., 2005), p. 126.

#94 David Hoffman, Little-Known FACTS about Well-Known PLACES Disneyland (New York: Metro Books, 2008), p. 43.

Kendra Trahan, Disneyland Detective: An INDEPENDENT Guide to Discovering Disney's Legend, Lore, and Magic! 50th Anniversary Update (Mission Viejo: PermaGrin Publishing, Inc., 2005), p. 126.

Smith, Dave, Chief Archivist Emeritus, Walt Disney Archives.

#95 The names of the six train engines are as follows:

1. I.B. Hearty
2. I.M. Brave
3. I.M. Bold
4. U.R. Courageous
5. U.R. Daring
6. U.R. Fearless

#96 Names of the Original Astro Jets:

1. Altair	4. Canopus	7. Procyon	10. Sirus
2. Antares	5. Capella	8. Regulus	11. Spica
3. Arcturus	6. Castor	9. Rigel	12. Vega

Chris Strodder, The Disneyland Encyclopedia: The UNOfficial, UNAuthorized, and UNPrecedented History of Every Land, Attraction, Restaurant, Shop, and Event in the Original Magic Kingdom (Santa Monica. Santa Monica Press LLC., 2008), p. 54.

#97 Names of the horse on King Arthur's Carrousel:

Findingmickey.com, Disneyland's King Arthur Carrousel Horses , http://findingmickey. squarespace.com/king-arthurs-carrousel-horses/ (10/1/2010).

Findingmickey.com, Disneyland's King Arthur Carrousel Horses , http://findingmickey. squarespace.com/king-arthurs-carrousel-horses/ (6/20/2012).

Findingmickey.com, Disneyland's King Arthur Carrousel Horses , http://findingmickey. squarespace.com/kac-horse-checklist/ (6/20/2012).

There are currently 85 horses listed in the official Disneyland's roster. King Arthur's Carrousel currently has 68 horses on it. The rest are in maintenance for repairs and/or maintence. They are rotated into service as others are taken out. Prior to 2003, there were 72 horse on King Arthur's Carrousel, but four were removed to add benchs to meet ADA requirements.

1. Alma	2. Arabian Knight	3. Atlantis
4. Avanti	5. Aztec	6. Baby
7. Bink	8. Blue	9. Brandy
10. Brittany Lee	11. Brittany's Rose	12. Bruce
13. Celeste	14. Centurion	15. Champion
16. Charlie	17. Checkers	18. Checkers Jr.

19. Cinch
20. Claudius
21. Cooper
22. Crusader
23. Dagger
24. Daisy
25. Dante
26. Debra Ann
27. Doubloon
28. Duke
29. Eagle Scout
30. Emerald
31. Fern
32. Flash
33. Flourish
34. Frenchy
35. Galaxy
36. Georgina
37. Gypsy
38. Hoot
39. Jester
40. Jingles (Lead)
41. Kaleidoscope
42. Keiffer
43. King
44. King Richard
45. Lance
46. Leo
47. Leprechaun
48. Liselotte
49. Looff
50. Lori Lyn
51. Lucifer's Rose
52. Lunatic
53. Lusco
54. M. W.
55. Marilyn
56. Marley
57. Mary Jane
58. Maurice
59. Merlin
60. National Velvet
61. Nipper
62. Pegasus
63. Penny
64. Queenie
65. Rally
66. Red Devil
67. Renaissance
68. Romance
69. Sage
70. Sapphire
71. Saxon
72. Screaming Eagle
73. Sea Biscuit
74 Sir Lancelot
75. St. Patrick
76. Tartan
77. Tassel
78. Testy Pat
79. Thistle
80. Tiny
81. Tulip
82. Uncle
83. Unice
84. Valance
85. Whiz Kid

Other names that were listed on prior lists but are no longer listed:

1. Belle
2. Chodis
3. Crown Jewel
4. Elinor
5. Elroy
6. Hal
7. Ivy
8. Patches
9. Steamer
10. Topaz
11. Turbo

#98 Jim Korkis, The Vault of Walt: Unofficial, Unauthorized, Uncensored Disney Stories Never Told (U.S.A.: Ayefour
Publishing, 2010), p. 289.

#99 Mike Calahan, High Ferality – Disneyland's Feral Cats. http://mikecalahan.com/?p=392 (November 9, 2010).

Ben Popken, Disneyland Partners With Feral Cat Colony To Control Rodents. http://consumerist.com/2010/09/disneyland-partners-with-feral-cat-colony-to-control-rodents.html (November 9, 2010)

#100 Chris Strodder, The Disneyland Encyclopedia: The UNOfficial, UNAuthorized, and UNPrecedented History of Every Land, Attraction, Restaurant, Shop, and Event in the Original Magic Kingdom (Santa Monica. Santa Monica Press LLC., 2008), p. 41.

#101 Chris Strodder, The Disneyland Encyclopedia: The UNOfficial, UNAuthorized, and UNPrecedented History of Every Land, Attraction, Restaurant, Shop, and Event in the Original Magic Kingdom (Santa Monica. Santa Monica Press LLC., 2008), p. 265.

#102 Jason Surrell, The Haunted Mansion: From Magic Kingdom to the Movies (New York. Disney Editions, 2003), p. 61.

Chris Strodder, The Disneyland Encyclopedia: The UNOfficial, UNAuthorized, and UNPrecedented History of Every Land, Attraction, Restaurant, Shop, and Event in the Original Magic Kingdom (Santa Monica. Santa Monica Press LLC., 2008), p. 204.

#103 Chris Strodder, The Disneyland Encyclopedia: The UNOfficial, UNAuthorized, and UNPrecedented History of Every Land, Attraction, Restaurant, Shop, and Event in the Original Magic Kingdom (Santa Monica. Santa Monica Press LLC., 2008), p. 86.

#104 Jason Surrell, Pirates of the Caribbean: From the Magic Kingdom to the Movies (New York. Disney Editions, 2005), p. 82.

Spacecoast's Hidden Mickeys of Disney, New Orleans Square Fun Facts, http://www.oitc.com/Disney/Disneyland/secrets/Square/Pirates.html (December 7, 2010).

#105 Kevin Yee and Jason Schultz, 101 Things You Never Knew About Disneyland: An Unauthorized Look at the Little Touches and Inside Jokes (Orlando: Zauberreich Press, 2005-2007), #48.

#106 Disney.com, Enviroport 2007: Annual Environmental Report for The Walt Disney Company, http://corporate.disney.go.com/environmentality/enviroport/2007/rc/aaf.html (9/28/2011).

#107 oitc.com, Fun Facts, http://www.oitc.com/Disney/Disneyland/secrets/Adventure/Jungle.html (9/28/2011).

1. Amazon Belle	8. Mekong Maiden (out of service)
2. Congo Queen	9. Nile Princess
3. Ganges Gal	10. Orinoco Adventuress
4. Hondo Hattie	11. Suwannee Lady
5. Irrawaddy Woman	12. Ucayali Una [Ucy]
6. Kissimmee Kate	13. Yangtze Lotus
7. Magdalena Maiden [Maggie] (out of service)	14. Zambezi Miss

#108 www.oitc.com, Fun Facts, http://www.oitc.com/Disney/disneyland/Secrets/Square/Pirates.html (#28) (9/28/2011).

freerepublic.com, 50 things you didn't know about Disneyland, http://www.freerepublic.com/focus/f-news/1528718/posts (#3) (9/28/2011).

disneylandreport.com, New Orleans Square Secrets and Facts, http://www.disneylandreport.com/disneysecrets/disneylandsecrets/neworleanssquaresecrets.html (9/28/2011).

#109 davelandweb.com, Fire Department/Walt's Apartment, http://davelandweb.com/townsquare/firedept.html (9/28/2011).

#110 The names of the Beehicles are as follows:

1. Blustery	12. Owl
2. Bother	13. Piglet
3. Bouncy	14. Pooh
4. Christopher Robin	15. Rabbit
5. Eeyore	16. Roo
6. Floody	17. Thotful
7. Gopher	18. Tigger
8. Heffabee	19. Tumbly
9. Heffalump	20. Rumbly (not confirmed)
10. Hunny	21. Winnie (Setup for special needs guests)
11. Mr. Sanders	22. Woozle (Setup for special needs guests)

#111 Allears.net, Many Adventures of Winnie the Pooh - Critter Country, Disneyland, http://allears.net/dlr/tp/dl/pooh.htm (1/22/2012).

#112 http://thedisneyblog.com, Star Tours – Inside Jokes, Tributes, Remnants, Homages, http://thedisneyblog.com/2011/06/03/star-tours-inside-jokes-tributes-remnants-homages/ (1/29/2012).

#113 LIST OF RESTROOMS:

1. To the left of the main entrance.
2. Main Street - Behind the Disney Gallery (formerly Annual Pass Guest Relations/Bank of America Building).
3. Main Street - To the right of City Hall.
4. Main Street - To the rear of Carnation Café.
5. Main Street - Baby Station.
6. Main Street - First Aid Station
7. Tomorrowland - Between Plaza Inn and Star Tours.
8. Tomorrowland - Exit to Space Mountain.
9. Tomorrowland - Between Autopia and Innoventions .
10. Fantasyland - In Castle behind Alice In Wonderland (on walkway between The Castle and Matterhorn).
11. Fantasyland - To right of Village Haus Restaurant (by Pinocchio's Daring Adventure).
12. Fantasyland - Entrance to Princess Fantasy Faire.
13. Toontown - Center of Toontown in garage.
14. Frontierland - To the right of the entrance to Rancho Zocalo's Restaurante.

15. Frontierland - Tom Sawyer/Pirates' Lair island in Ft. Wilderness (to right of main gates).
16. Frontierland - Tom Sawyer/Pirates' Lair island at Water Wheel (opposite end of island from Ft. Wilderness).
17. Frontierland - The left of the small stage at the Big Thunder Ranch Bar-B-Que.
18. Adventureland - In the intersection between Tiki Room, Pioneer Mercantile and South Seas Traders.
19. Adventureland—In the Tiki Room.
20. Adventureland - Aladdin's Oasis (This is currently being used as the family restroom).
21. Adventureland - Half way through the queue of Indiana Jones (This is a Cast member restroom and it is not generally open to public, but desperate guests can ask a cast member. Usually not counted)
22. New Orleans Square - Club 33 (Open to members and their guests only).
23. New Orleans Square - Blue Bayou Restaurant (open to patrons of the restaurant).
24. New Orleans Square - To the left of the New Orleans' Train Station.
25. Critter Country - Under the Hungry Bear Restaurant.

Chris Strodder, The Disneyland Encyclopedia: The UNOfficial, UNAuthorized, and UNPrecedented History of Every Land, Attraction, Restaurant, Shop, and Event in the Original Magic Kingdom (Santa Monica. Santa Monica Press LLC., 2008), p. 353 – 355.

MousePlanet.com, The Happiest Potties On Earth. http://www.mouseplanet.com/potties/ijtferestroom.html?148,94 (May 21, 2010).

#114 There are approximatelly 1250 trash cans at Disneyland.

Dave Smith, Disney Trivia from the Vault: Secrets Revealed and Questions Answered (New York, Disney Editions, 2012), p. 83.

#115 Jeff Baham, An Unofficial History of Disney's Haunted Mansion (United States of America, Doombuggies.com, 2010), p. 29.

#116 There are 131 Boombuggies, they run on a 786 foot long track that loops. They travel at a normal speed of 1.36 miles per hour and can move 2,618 guests through the attraction per hour.

Jeff Baham, An Unofficial History of Disney's Haunted Mansion (United States of America, Doombuggies.com, 2010), p. 60.

#117 Smith, Dave, Chief Archivist Emeritus, Walt Disney Archives.

Gurr, Robert (Bob), Author and former Imagineer.

BIBLIOGRAPHY

BOOKS

Baham, Jeff. An Unofficial History of Disney's Haunted Mansion . United States: Doombuggies.com, 2010.

Barrett, Steven M. Disneyland's Hidden Mickeys: A Field Guide to Disneyland Resort's Best Kept Secrets . Bradford, CT: The Intrepid Traveler, 2007.

Cotter, Bill. The Wonderful World of Disney Television: The Complete History . New York: Hyperion, 1997.

Disneyland: Dreams, Traditions and Transitions . USA: The Walt Disney Company, 1995.

Disneyland: Memories of a Lifetime . New York: Disney Editions, 2000.

Disneyland: The First Quarter Century . Burbank, CA: Walt Disney Productions, 1979.

Disneyland Resort: Magical Memories for a Lifetime . New York: Disney Editions, 2002.

Dunham, M.L. and Lara Bergen. Disney Junior Encyclopedia of Animated Characters: Includes characters from your favorite Disney PIXAR films . New York: Disney Press, 2009.

Finch, Christopher. The Art of Walt Disney: From Mickey Mouse to the Magic Kingdoms . Burbank, CA: Walt Disney Productions, 1975.

Flanning, Jim. Disneyland Challenge .New York: Disney Editions, Inc., 2009.

Gordon, Bruce and Tim O'Day. Disneyland: Then, Now, and Forever , New York: Disney Editions, Inc., 2005.

Gordon, Bruce and Tim O'Day. Disneyland: Then, Now, and Forever , New York: Disney Editions, Inc., 2008.

Green, Amy Boothe and Howard E. Green. Remembering Walt: Favorite Memories of Walt Disney , New York: Disney Editions, Inc., 1999.

Hahn, Don. The Alchemy of Animation: Making an Animated Film in the Modern Age . New York: Disney Editions, Inc., 2008.

Hench, John with Peggy Van Pelt. Designing Disney: Imagineering and the Art of the Show . New York: Disney Editions, Inc., 2008.

Hoffman, David. Little-Known FACTS about Well-Known PLACES Disneyland .New York: Metro Books, 2008.

Jacobs, David. Disney's America on Parade: A History of the U.S.A. in a Dazzling, Fun-Filled Pageant . New York: Harry N. Abrams, Inc., 1975.

Kaufman, J. B.. The Walt Disney Family Museum: The Man, The Magic, The Memories . New York: Disney Editions, 2009.

Koenig, David. More Mouse Tales: A Closer Peek Backstage At Disneyland .Irvine, CA: Bonaventure Press, 1999/2002.

Koenig, David. Mouse Tales: A Behind-The-Ears Look At Disneyland .Irvine, CA: Bonaventure Press, 1994/1995/2006.

Koenig, David. Mouse Under Glass: Secrets of Disney Animation and Theme Parks .Irvine, CA: Bonaventure Press, 1997/2001.

Korkis, Jim. The Vault of Walt: Unofficial, Unauthorized, Uncensored Disney Stories Never Told .U.S.A.: Ayefour Publishing, 2100.

Kurtti, Jeff. Disney Dossiers: Files of Character From The Walt Disney Studios . New York: Disney Enterprises, Inc., 2006.

Kurtti, Jeff. Walt Disney's Imagineering Legends and the Genesis of the Disney Theme Park . New York: Disney Editions, 2008.

Kurtti, Jeff. DISNEYLAND: From Once Upon A Time To Happily Ever After . New York: Disney Editions, 2010.

Kurtti, Jeff. DISNEYLAND Through The Decades: A Photographic Celebration . New York: Disney Editions, 2010

Lanzarini, Lisa, ed. Disney: The Ultimate Visual Guide . New York: DK, 2002.

Yee, Kevin and Jason Schultz. 101 Things You Never Knew About Disneyland: An Unauthorized Look at the Little Touches and Inside Jokes .Orlando, FL: Zauberreich Press, 2005-2007.

Lefkon, Wendy. Birnbaum's 2003 Disneyland Resort: Expert Advice from the Inside Source. New York: Disney Editions, Inc., 2003.

Lefkon, Wendy, ed. The Imagineering Field Guide to Disneyland: An Imagineer's-Eye Tour . New York: Disney Editions, Inc., 2008.

Lefkon, Wendy, ed. Walt Disney Imagineering: A Behind the Dreams Look at Making the Magic Real . New York: Hyperion, 1996.

Malmberg, Melody, ed. Walt Disney Imagineering: A Behind the Dreams Look at Making MORE Magic Real . New York: Disney Editions, 2010.

Marling, Karal Ann. Behind The Magic: 50 Years of Disneyland . Dearborn, MI: Henry Ford Museum, 2004.

Mosley, Leonard. Disney's World . Lanham, MD: Scarborough House, 1990.

O'Day, Tim, Jody Revenson, Lorraine Santoli, Leonard Shannon, The Imagineers, and Wendy Lefkon, ed. Disneyland Resort: Remember the Moments, A Magical Souvenir . New York: Disney Enterprises, Inc, 2005.

O'Day, Tim, Lorraine Santoli, and Wendy Lefkon, ed. Disneyland Resort: A Pictorial Souvenir . New York: Disney Editions, 2002.

Picture Souvenir Book of Disneyland in Natural Color . New York: Disney Editions, 1955/2005.

Preszler, June. Walt Disney . Mankato, MN: Bridgestone Books, 2003.

Schroeder, Russell K. Disney: The Ultimate Visual Guide . New York: DK Publishing, 2002.

Schroeder, Russell, ed. Walt Disney: His Life In Pictures . New York: Disney Press, 2009.

Selden, Bernice. The Story of Walt Disney, Maker of Magical Worlds . New York: Yearling, 1989.

Sklar, Martin A. Walt Disney's Disneyland . USA: Walt Disney Productions, 1969.

Sklar, Martin A. Walt Disney's Disneyland . USA: Walt Disney Productions, 1969 (updated with material through 1975).

Smith, Dave. Disney A to Z: The Official Encyclopedia (Third Edition). New York: Disney Editions, 2006

Smith, Dave. Disney A to Z: The Updated Official Encyclopedia. New York: Hyperion, 1996.

Smith, Dave: Disney Trivia from the Vault: Secrets Revealed and Questions Answered. New York: Disney Editions, 2012.

Smith, Dave and Steven Clark. Disney: The First 100 Years (Updated Edition), New York: Disney Enterprises, Inc., 2002.

Snyder, Chuck. Windows On Main Street: Discover the Real Stories of the Talented People Featured on the Windows of Main Street, U.S.A. . New York: Disney Editions, Inc., 2009.

Stewart, Whitney. Who Was Walt Disney? . New York: Penguin Group (USA), Inc., 2009.

Strodder, Chris. The Disneyland Encyclopedia: The UNOfficial, UNAuthorized, and UNPrecedented History of Every Land, Attraction, Restaurant, Shop, and Event in the Original Magic Kingdom . Santa Monica, CA: Santa Monica Press LLC., 2008.

Surrell, Jason. Pirates of the Caribbean: From the Magic Kingdom to the Movies . New York: Disney Editions, Inc., 2005.

Surrell, Jason. The Disney Mountains: Imagineering at its Peak . New York: Disney Editions, Inc., 2007.

Surrell, Jason. The Haunted Mansion: From the Magic Kingdom to the Movies . New York: Disney Editions, Inc., 2003.

Sutcliffe, Jane. Walt Disney . New York: Barnes and Noble, 2009.

Thie, Carlene. A Photographer's Life with Disneyland Under Construction . Riverside, CA: Ape Pen Publishing Company, 2002.

Thie, Carlene. Disney Years: Seen Through a Photographer's Lens . Riverside, CA: Ape Pen Publishing Company, 2002.

Thie, Carlene. Disney's Early Years: Through the Eye of a Photographer . Riverside, CA: Ape Pen Publishing Company, 2002.

Thomas, Bob. Disney's Art of Animation From Mickey Mouse To Beauty and the Beast . New York: Hyperion, 1991.

Trahan, Kendra. Disneyland Detective: An INDEPENDENT Guide to Discovering Disney's Legend, Lore, and Magic! . Mission Viejo, CA: PermaGrin Publishing, Inc., 2005.

Walt Disney's Comics and Stories: No. 688 January 2008. USA: Gemstone Publishing, 2008.

Walt Disney's Disneyland: A Pictorial Souvenir . USA: Walt Disney Productions, 1976.

Walt Disney's Guide to Disneyland 9th Edition . USA: Walt Disney Productions , 1964.

Walt Disney's The Original Disneyland: Pictorial Souvenir New 1993 Edition . USA: The Walt Disney Company, 1993.

Williams, Pat with Jim Denney. How to be Like Walt Disney: Capturing the Disney Magic Every Day of Your Life . Deerfield, FL: Health Communications, Inc. , 2004.

Wolf, Scott and Shani Wolf. Where in Disneyland Park? . Burbank, CA: Page Publishing, 1994.

Zibart, Eve. Today in History: Disney . Cincinnati, OH: Emmis Books, 2006.

MAGAZINES (No specific articles were used but many magazines were reviewed)
D23

Disney Family Fun.

Disney Files Magazine.

Disney Insider

Disney Magazine.

Disney Rewards.

Disneyland Back Stage Pass.

Disneyland Resort: Annual Passholder News.

E Ticket

INTERNET
Allears.net. (n.d.). Big Thunder Mountain Railroad - Frontierland, Disneyland. Retrieved January 22, 2012, from http://allears.net/dlr/tp/dl/btmrr.htm

Allears.net. (n.d.). Cinderella Castle - Magic Kingdom. Retrieved September 29, 2010, from http://allears.net/tp/mk/castle.htm

Allears.net. (n.d.). Many Adventures of Winnie the Pooh - Critter Country, Disneyland. Retrieved January 22, 2012, from http://allears.net/dlr/tp/dl/pooh.htm

Baham, Jeff. (2009, June 30). 5 Disneyland secrets that nobody knows. Retrieved April 23, 2010, from http://www.examiner.com/x-10719-Disney-Theme-Parks-Examiner~y2009m6d30-5-Disneyland-secrets-that-nobody-knows

Brunner, Borgna and Mark Hughes. (n.d.). Presidential Pardon: The turkey that lives to see another day. Retrieved April 23, 2010, from http://www.infoplease.com/spot/tgturkey2.html

Bumiller, Elisabeth. (2005, November 23). Two Turkeys Pardoned, With First-Class Tickets. Retrieved September 28, 2010, from http://www.nytimes.com/2005/11/23/national/23bush.html?_r=1&scp=1&sq=Two%20Turkeys%20Pardoned,%20With%20First-Class%20Tickets&st=cse

Cey, Janet. (2009, September 23). 5 Fun Trivia Facts About Disneyland. Retrieved September 28, 2010, from Silvester, William. Disney's Sleeping Beauty Castle. Retrieved September 29, 2010, from http://www.suite101.com/content/sleeping-beauty-castle-a47210

Daveland.com. (n.d.). Daveland Disneyland Astrojets Photo Page. Retrieved September, 29, 2010, from http://davelandweb.com/astrojets/

Daveland.com. (2009, February 3). Daveland@Disneyland A-Z: Adventureland Gate. Retrieved May 4, 2010, from http://www.2719hyperion.com/2009/02/davelanddisneyland-in-photos-az.html

Daveland.com. (2009, June 18). Tell-No-Tales Thursdays: Entrance Queue Mural. Retrieved June 18, 2010, from http://davelandblog.blogspot.com/2009/06/tell-no-tales-thursdays-entrance-queue.html

Disboard.com. (2008, February 12). My Favorite Secrets. Retrieved September 5, 2010, from http://www.disboards.com/showthread.php?t=989311&page=7

Daveland.com (n.d.). Fire Department/Walt's Apartment. Retrieved September 28, 2011, from http://davelandweb.com/townsquare/firedept.html

Daveland.com (n.d.). Sleeping Beauty Diorama. Retrieved July 19, 2010, from http://davelandweb.com/castle/diorama.html

Disney.com (n.d.). Enviroport 2007: Annual Environmental Report for The Walt Disney Company. Retrieved September 28, 2011, from http://corporate.disney.go.com/environmentality/enviroport/2007/rc/aaf.html

Disney.wikia.com. (n.d.). Disneyland Railroad. Retrieved October 3, 2010, from http://disney.wiki.com/wiki/Disneyland_Railroad

Disney.wikia.com. (n.d.). Minnie Mouse. Retrieved September 27, 2010, from http://disney.wikia.com/wiki/Minnie_Mouse

Disneylandnews.com. (n.d.). Disneyland Fun Facts. Retrieved September 28, 2010, from http://www.disneylandnews.com/fact+sheets+and+more/background/disneyland+park+fun+facts.htm

Disneylandclub33.com. (n.d.). How Do I Join?. Retrieved September 25, 2010, from http://www.disneylandclub33.com/How-Do_I-Join.htm

Disneylandclub33.com. (n.d.). Welcome To Our Club 33 Home Page. Retrieved September 25, 2010, from http://www.disneylandclub33.com/index.html

disneylandreport.com. (n.d.). New Orleans Square Secrets and Facts. Retrieved September 28, 2011, from http://www.disneylandreport.com/disneysecrets/disneylandsecrets/neworleanssquaresecrets.html

Disney-pal.com (n.d.). The Many Adventures of Winnie the Pooh. Retrieved January 19, 2012, from http://www.disney-pal.com/Disneyland/many_adventures_of_winnie_fun_facts.htm

Eldridge, George. (n.d.). Decoding the Disneyland Telegraph. Retrieved April 23, 2010, from http://www.hiddenmickeys.org/Disneyland/Secrets/Square/Morse.html

Facebook.com. (n.d.). Minnie Mouse. Retrieved September 28, 2010, from http://www.facebook.com/#!/pages/Minnie-Mouse/112067295472969?ref=ts

FindingMickey.com. (n.d.). Disneyland Facts & History > Main Street U. S. A.. Retrieved September 29, 2010, from http://findingmickey.squarespace.com/disneyland-facts/main-street-usa/

Findingmickey.com. (2010). Disneyland's King Arthur Carrousel Horses. Retrieved October 1, 2010, from http://findingmickey.squarespace.com/king-arthurs-carrousel-horses/

Findingmickey.com. (2012). Disneyland's King Arthur Carrousel Horses. Retrieved June 20, 2012, from http://findingmickey.squarespace.com/king-arthurs-carrousel-horses/

Findingmickey.com. (2012). Disneyland's Official - King Arthur Carrousel Horse Roster. Retrieved June 20, 2012, from http://findingmickey.squarespace.com/kac-horse-checklist/

Freerepublic.com. (n.d.). 50 things you didn't know about Disneyland. Retrieved September 28, 2011, from http://www.freerepublic.com/focus/f-news/1528718/posts

Google. General Searches, www.google.com (Various).

Hart, Alexander C. (2009, November 26). Pardoned turkeys off to Disneyland. Retrieved September 28, 2010, from http://articles.latimes.com/2009/nov/26/nation/la-na-turkey-pardon26-2009nov26

HiddenMickeys.org. (n.d.). Fun Facts of Disneyland's Sleeping Beauty Castle. Retrieved September 28, 2010, from http://www.hiddenmickeys.org/Disneyland/Secrets/Fantasy/Castle.html

MiceChat.com. (2005, April 29). What was the Observatron. Retrieved September 29, 2010, from http://micechat.com/forums/disneyland-resort/3475-what-observatron.html

Mickeypedia.com. (n.d.). Minnie Mouse. Retrieved September 27, 2010, from http://www.mickeypedia.com/articles/Disney/Minnie_Mouse.html

MouseBuzz.com. (2010, September 25). Secret bathroom at DL?. Retrieved September 25, 2010, from http://www.mousebuzz.com/forum/disneyland-theme-parks/49179-secret-bathroom-dl.html

MousePlanet.com. (2010, April 8). I need a picture of the entry/walkway to the secret bathroom!. Retrieved September 29, 2010, from http://mousepad.mouseplanet.com/

showthread.php?t=144399&highlight=secret+bathroom

MousePlanet.com. (n.d.). The Happiest Potties On Earth. Retrieved May 21, 2010, from http://www.mouseplanet.com/potties/ijtferestroom.html?148,94

MousePlanet.com. (n.d.). The Secret Bathroom. Retrieved September 25, 2010, from http://mousepad.mouseplanet.com/showthread.php?t=53169&goto=nextoldest

Nirattisai, Preston. (2008). A Different Look At Disney. Retrieved July 16, 2010, from http://miceage.micechat.com/stevedegaetano/sd102308a.htm

Oceanic Arts. (2010, May 3). Humuhumu's Description. Retrieved May 3, 2010, from http://www.critiki.com/cgi-bin/location.cgi?loc_id=202

oitc.com. (n.d.). Fun Facts. Retrieved September 28, 2011, from http://www.oitc.com/Disney/Disneyland/secrets/Adventure/Jungle.html

oitc.com. (n.d.). Fun Facts. Retrieved September 28, 2011, from http://www.oitc.com/Disney/disneyland/Secrets/Square/Pirates.html

Silvester, William. (2008, March 10). Disney's Sleeping Beauty Castle. Retrieved September 29, 2010, from http://www.suite101.com/content/sleeping-beauty-castle-a47210

Thedisneyblog.com (2011, June 30). Star Tours – Inside Jokes, Tributes, Remnants, Homages. Retrieved January 29, 2012, from http://thedisneyblog.com/2011/06/03/star-tours-inside-jokes-tributes-remnants-homages/

Tiki Central. (2004, January 17). Oceanic Arts, Whittier, CA . Retrieved May, 4, 2010, from http://www.tikiroom.com/tikicentral/bb/viewtopic.php?topic=7252&forum=2

Ultimaterollercoaster.com. (n.d.). Matterhorn Bobsleds Roller Coaster. Retrieved September 27, 2010, from http://www.ultimaterollercoaster.com/coasters/yellowpages/coasters/matterhorn_disneyl.shtml

Visionsfantastic.com. (2010, September 25). Secret Bathroom. Retrieved September 25, 2010, from http://www.visionsfantastic.com/forum/f52/secret-bathroom-9492/

Wallace, David. (2007, September 7). Disneyland Trivia: Walt Disney's Apartment. Retrieved September 29, 2010, from http://www.davidwallace.com/2007/09/disneyland-trivia-walt-disneys-apartment/

Wikipedia.com. (n.d.). Disneyland Railroad,. Retrieved May 9, 2010, from http://en.wikipedia.org/wiki/Disneyland_Railroad

Yesterdayland.com. (2010, September 29). Rocket Jets at Yesterland. Retrieved September 29, 2010, from http://www.yesterland.com/rocketjets.html

DISNEY LANGUAGE

Attraction: Any ride or show.

Cast Member: An employee of the Disney Company. This carries from the philosophy that Disneyland is like a mulit-demensional movie expereince.

D23: The Official Disney Fan Club.

DVC: Disney Vacation Club.

Guest: Most businesses refer to patrons as customers. Disney refers to its patrons as Guest to foster an attitude and feeling of how they want Cast Members to treat their patrons.

Hidden Mickey: The set of three circles that generaly form the shape of a classic Mickey Mouse head. Some are obvious, while others take some looking.

Imagineer: A person who works for Walt Disney Imagineering. This word is a combination of Imagination and Engineer. They are part storyteller, part viusual artist, and part engineer.

Imagineering: Short for Walt Disney Imagineering.

Park or The Park; A shortened reference to the Disneyland Park.

Plus, Plus It, or Plussing: That is where Disney refurbishes, upgrades, adds to an attractions or in some way changes an attraction to make it more enjoyable for guests.

Queue: A line you stand in for an attraction, food or entry/exit.

Re-purposed: To reuse an item after it is no longer needed in its current function. The item may be used in whole or in part. It could even be modified.

Themed: The central idea or concept for an attraction or area.

Tribute: Where an object or reference is incorporated into a new attraction to show respect for a previous attraction. Tributes are often used where one attraction replaces another one.

Walt Disney Imagineering: The department within of the Disney family of companies that is responsible for the designand maintenance attractions found in the Parks.

WED: The forerunner to Walt Disney Imagineering. Originally formed from Walt Disney's staff from the Walt Disney Studio. The acronym stands for Walter Elias Disney.